Odette Deprés Chase

This Child's War

A World War II Memoir

Odette Depres Chase

Red Bud Publishing Company
Lebanon, Indiana

© Copyright 2004 Odette Depres Chase

No part of this book may be reproduced or transmited in any form or by any means, electronic or mechanical, including photocopying, recording, or by any information storage and retrieval system, without permission in writing from the following:

Red Bud Publishing Co.
2425 Lakeshore Court
Lebanon, Indiana 46052

ISBN: 0-9759421-0-7

Dedication

To My Parents

Foreword

I raised my children telling them war stories instead of fairy tales, because this was all I knew. One of my sons, still fascinated by it all even after he grew up, urged me to write those war memories down, before I would completely forget about them. I finally consented, and to my surprise, it felt good to relive the past and rediscover the child I used to be. This is my story. It is the true survival story of my entire family during World War II, in France, under Nazi occupation. It could be anyone's story living in Europe at that time.

The war robbed me of a carefree childhood and certainly tainted my teenage years as well. In fact, it affected me for the rest of my life. Going to bed hungry every night for nearly five years, I have great difficulty to this day in throwing hard (or even spoiled) bread away. I give it to the birds. It feels less sinful. Deprived of every single little item, like paper bags or soap or warm socks, I salvage and recycle or find some other use for nearly everything. Laughter is something my children had to teach me again. I grew old in childhood. So did all the other children around me. We had so many responsibilities then, we were developing wisdom.

In this book, I hope, you will find a story of courage and endurance and determination. My parents happened to be poor, extremely poor, which of course aggravated the situation, but their story is typical of many other French families in my town or even in the entire nation of France, during the Nazi occupation of 1940 till 1945. And I am so proud of my countrymen who fought so valiantly then, and even gave their lives so their children could live free again.

I came to the United States in 1956 with my American husband and a fifteen month old little boy. All at once, I was thrilled by the novelty of things, the stores full of items that I wanted to buy, the pretty houses and the comfort of modern plumbing. Nevertheless, I quickly became homesick. I missed my family, I missed my country and the lifestyle of French people who love to congregate for long talks. My husband remedied all that by sponsoring my sister first, then my parents, and we all created a home away from home.

I now live in Lebanon, Indiana, a little town located just a few miles north of Indianapolis, a lovely city I discovered by accident when traveling through the Midwest after separation from my husband and then abruptly chose to stay there.

"A good place to raise a family," my inner voice told me then, loud and clear. Besides, the weeds growing alongside the road strangely resembled those growing in my village back in France. So, for over thirty years, Indianapolis became the hub where I worked and my children grew up. Now, Lebanon, a quieter place, welcomes me each time I come home after visiting friends or babysitting for my grandchildren. Here and there, a flight to France renews my spirit.

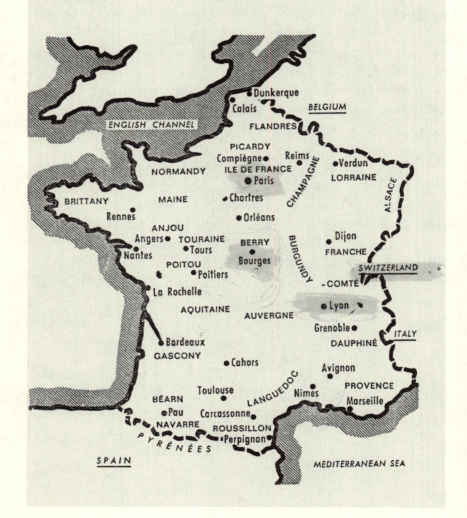

Chapter 1

When the Germans Came

"Bourges is declared Open City," someone shouted at my father. "The Germans are marching down fast," screamed another. "We are leaving! The whole town is leaving," added somebody else, pointing to the crowd down the street.

My parents and I stood outside our doorway, bewildered by what was happening in our neighborhood, our town, our country. The words Open City bounced from group to group. By the reaction on the people's faces, I knew it meant something horrifying.

It was late spring 1940, I was barely nine years old, and the German army was invading my country, France. I remember the panic that spread everywhere. People fled on foot, on bicycles or in their small cars, and crowded the roads going south. Mothers pushed baby carriages while other children tagged along at their sides; older men and women followed painfully with their most precious possessions bundled in a hurry and piled in wheelbarrows. They formed an exodus of frightened people running away from German soldiers; all were trying desperately to reach an imaginary line which supposedly would divide free France from Nazi-occupied France. Eventually all of France became occupied.

Those who stayed behind met in groups, on sidewalks and in courtyards, in front of opened windows where owners of radios kept the sound loud enough for everyone to hear the latest news. With complete consternation, they learned that Italy, abruptly allied with Germany, had begun relentless attacks on our highways, killing thousands of helpless French civilians on their way to safety.

I was the oldest of three children. My brother, Michel, was a year younger than I, while my sister, Lucienne, was born four years later. My father worked in a factory, and my mother stayed home as a housewife. We lived on the top floor of a three-story building in the center of town, off a narrow cobblestone street, with no electricity and no running water. An older lady, widowed and all alone in the world after her two sons left for war and never returned, had joined our household a few months before the birth of my baby sister. She prepared our breakfast each morning on our wood-burning stove: café au lait, crusty bread, butter and jam. She also baked cherry tarts and made great omelets. My siblings and I respectfully called her *Grand-mère* (Grandmother), to her delight.

My parents, not knowing where else to go with three young children and an elderly woman while so many others fled, decided to wait quietly behind closed doors and face whatever would happen. My mother accumulated a supply of food to last us a couple of months and tucked it away in a large basket under the bed. The stores closed down, the factories did the same, and my father found himself out of work. The streets looked deserted.

And so the Germans came. Curious to know what "Germans" really looked like, I sneaked out from our apartment one day, ran down three flights of stairs in complete darkness, opened an outside courtyard door and peeked into the street. Nothing. I was greatly disappointed—but not for long!

I do not know the exact moment the German tanks rolled into my town. Maybe they came at night while I slept or during the day when my mother kept me away from the window, but when I finally stepped outside, German soldiers stood everywhere: they patrolled my street, visited my school, inspected our grocery stores, and controlled our factories. Armed men in green uniforms marching like invincible robots, shining black boots that hit the pavement so hard people and ground trembled, orders shouted in a language that I did not understand: those are the undying images imprinted in my memory of the German army taking over my town. Petrified by the sight and sound of those menacing warriors, I forever kept a low profile any time I encountered soldiers later on.

People we thought to be French, like my father's supervisor at his work place, appeared overnight dressed in German military uniforms. Had they been spies all along? Summoned to a government office building to receive our food ration cards, we unwillingly released the names, ages and addresses of all family members. Whoever owned weapons was instructed to turn them in immediately. A curfew was established, and anyone caught wandering in the streets at night would be shot on the spot. A clerk counseled us to carry identification papers on us at all times or risk being arrested. Forbidden to leave town, we could not freely travel any more. Special permits would be granted only in cases of extreme urgency. This new regulation meant I could no longer hop on the local train and visit my grandmother who lived in a small village about sixty kilometers away. I loved both my grandparents who made me feel so secure in their little house, and I already missed them.

In a matter of days, our life turned into terror. At night, we darkened our windows and the bottoms of doors with heavy blankets to stop the light from escaping. The town had to be plunged into total darkness so the "enemy" planes (English, Canadian, and later, American) could not easily find their targets. A friend of ours carelessly forgot this new rule and almost lost her life. Getting up in the middle of the night to use the bathroom, she turned the light switch on and failed to notice her window was not properly camouflaged. A few seconds later a bullet crashed in, shattered the light bulb, and lodged itself in the wall. A German guard on duty by her building swiftly warned her never to forget again. The rules were clear and had to be followed. Anyone defying them would be shot, or worse, handed over to the Gestapo—the Nazi secret police. The Gestapo tortured people, always! The Gestapo blocked an entire street a few blocks away from our home by the main Post Office building and did not let anyone go through the barricades without a special pass. All the neighboring buildings were requisitioned and transformed into German Police headquarters. At night, people living nearby heard the sound of human screams seeping through the thick walls.

During the day, we endured all kinds of rules and restrictions. At night, we ran to shelters because of air raids. Trains no longer arrived on time at their destination. Planes appeared with little warning and dropped their bombs with deadly aim on anything that moved.

Then there was hunger—a terrible hunger. The Germans commandeered our food to feed their own soldiers first. The rest would be divided among the French population. Basic items that used to be plentiful like potatoes, bread, eggs and dairy products became scarce. Our rations were pitifully small. A squabble erupted once at the dinner table in my home over a ration of bread: my brother, Michel, strong, healthy, growing and constantly hungry, wanted twice as much while my father, needing his strength to work at the factory, was reluctant to share his portion. My mother gave her own portion away, dividing it between the two men.

French people, known to make good bread, normally eat large amounts of it. But during the war, not only was our bread rationed, it did not even taste good. Dark, coarse, indigestible, made of leftover grains and I don't know what else (sawdust, I heard), it caused hundreds of people to get sick, myself included. I developed ugly, purulent sores inside my hands and between my fingers. *La gale de pain,* people called the disease. Once a week, I visited a small clinic run by Catholic nuns who carefully cleaned my wounds and changed my bandages but could not stop the infection. I eventually gave up eating the bread altogether as it was slowly poisoning me. My brother, happy to have double rations, thrived on it.

The search for food never ended. Going to bed hungry every night, I dreamt of potatoes, bread, and thick slices of meat. One summer day, as my stomach hurt more than usual, I scavenged down the street and collected all the peach pits laying in the gutter. Taking them home, I broke them open one by one, and spent hours eating the seeds inside, savoring every bite slowly.

Some German soldiers felt sorry for the starving children. Their own families probably did not fare much better back home in Germany. I remember one instance, while I played outside with two or three of my friends, a German soldier strolled by nonchalantly munching on a bag of peanuts. By accident, he dropped a few on the ground. In no time, we were on the spot, grabbing and fighting over the peanuts. The commotion made the soldier turn around and have a look. In a glance he realized what was happening and, without a word, dropped the whole pack at his feet and slowly moved away. Maybe he had children of his own and felt compassion for us.

My health was deteriorating rapidly. By then I was dangerously anemic. Either I did not have enough to eat, or the food did not agree with me. Also the air was foul with bad odors most of the time. A little stream swirling through town passed directly by our courtyard and my whole neighborhood used it as a sewage and garbage disposal.

Because of the pollution in the area, the turmoil of war, the lack of food and fresh air, our family doctor grew very pessimistic about my survival. He recommended we move away from the town and wrote papers to that effect. My parents, following his suggestion, rushed to seek permission from German authorities. Then, by some astonishing accomplishment, we found ourselves moving to a new house far in the countryside, leaving the war and the German soldiers behind. Or so we thought . . . .

Chapter 2

Living in the Country during the War

The highway finally made a turn and there, amidst the greenery of trees and bushes, the house stood big, bright, like a splash of white, and radiant with sunshine. A small creek trickled down over sparkling pebbles and across a vegetable garden before being washed into a pond.

We heard birds singing. Behind the house and the trees, fields of golden wheat rolled as far as the eyes could see. Michel and I stared spellbound, unable to move or speak, completely awed, sitting still in the wagon that carried our family and all our belongings, long after the horses had pulled into the driveway and stopped.

We had left the city hours before, moving slowly under the shade of large trees into a land of green pastures and yellow crops. Along the way, we had seen cows, horses, sheep and farmers at work. Gently rocked by the even rhythm and sound of the horses' hooves on the asphalt, my little sister, Lucienne, had fallen asleep. I had kept my eyes opened, completely mesmerized by all the new country sights in this late summer afternoon.

My father's voice shook us from our thoughts: "Let's go, time to unload." Still in disbelief, Michel and I jumped down to the ground and rushed to explore the inside of the house. We discovered a huge sunny kitchen with high ceilings and large windows, a smaller and darker room in back, and three bedrooms upstairs with shiny white walls. So much light!

"We surely will not miss our old dark apartment," I exclaimed, "or the long walk down three flights of stairs to get water," I continued, as my father pointed out the well that stood only a few yards away.

Even the knowledge of another family moving into the rest of the building, as the house served as a double, did not tarnish our joy. The excitement of the day and the fresh air mixed with the scent of wildflowers put us fast asleep that first night. Later in the week, Michel and I forced ourselves to stay awake so we could marvel at the night sky filled with stars.

As we had hoped, my father found work on a farm nearby and the farmer rewarded him with extra milk, eggs, and cheese. The village bakery, whose bread tasted as good as it smelled, continuously gave us more than our rations. Hunger subsided. The sores on my fingers vanished, and the nuns at the clinic would have called it a miracle. There, in the remote countryside, the war all at once seemed to be far away. But, of course, it was not.

As Michel and I played in the front yard one day, we heard a rumbling sound coming from the road: an uproar of loud voices, heavy steps and the rattling of machinery. Puzzled, we crouched at the edge of tall grass and waited quietly. Soon, an army of German soldiers filed in front of us, in full gear with helmets, guns, and combat boots that hit the ground so hard we felt the earth shake beneath us. Divided in small groups that shouted in cadence, they marched erect, almost rigid, forceful and unstoppable, as if made of steel. A convoy of trucks followed them, carrying equipment—cannons whose barrels stuck out from underneath their cloth covers. We stayed silent long after the last truck had disappeared, feeling threatened and afraid to move.

A few days later my father, who routinely walked through his garden early in the morning before going to work, noticed a gun lying on a patch of land he had cleared the night before. Mystified, he resisted the impulse to pick up the weapon, knowing that the possession of firearms meant arrest and interrogation by the Gestapo. The Gestapo invariably tortured people to extract more information. My father had to dispose of the gun swiftly. Throwing dirt and debris over it, he hauled the whole heap into his wheelbarrow, which he slowly pushed toward the creek. Emptying his load into the current, he watched it sink down. We never found the reason why or how the gun had landed in our garden.

The school Michel, Lucienne and I attended during this time in the countryside stood over two kilometers away. We walked the distance twice a day, carrying lunches that we warmed up in wintertime on a coal-burning stove placed in the center of the classroom. The village and its surroundings drew just enough students ranging in age from six to fourteen years old to occupy two classrooms, keeping boys and girls separated according to custom. Our teachers, a young married couple, lived on the premises and taught the children of their own gender.

One Sunday at noon, Michel and I met our father at the farm where he worked that morning, and as we were returning home with him, we stumbled into a group of men standing in a clearing next to the woods. Engaged in a deep conversation and looking down at a map sprawled at their feet on the ground, they jumped when they heard our familiar "Bonjour," then hurriedly folded their papers and seemed suddenly absorbed in the details of an overgrown plant. Obviously, we had surprised and disturbed them, so we quickly stopped the chatting and continued on our way. We recognized one of the men–Michel's teacher–and we wondered what he was doing so far away from the schoolhouse. My father, silent for a few minutes, told us it would be best to forget this encounter and furthermore, never again use this shortcut!

Rumors of an underground movement referred to as *Le Maquis* surfaced nearly every day. French soldiers who refused to surrender to the German army fled into remote parts of the country to hide. Young men and women followed them in greater number. Eventually, they developed an organization called the Resistance, an amazing network of anonymous people who fought the Germans any way they could. They ambushed enemy patrols, sabotaged railroads to slow down the flow of French goods to Germany, spied on enemy military installations and relayed the information by radio to London. The Resistance lifted our spirits. The Resistance was our country's only hope, it seemed. Everyone pulled together to help its cause by providing food and shelter wherever and whenever possible. We were certain we had just witnessed a clandestine meeting of Maquisards, as we called these brave men. A few months later, we learned with sadness that the Gestapo had arrested our teacher.

Because of the vast territory under its control and the many battles still being fought on several fronts, Germany drafted most of its male population into its gigantic army, thus creating an acute labor shortage on the homeland. The number of prisoners of war forced to work on German farms, factories, hospitals and labor camps proved insufficient. German officials began urging each French young man to volunteer and replace one of our prisoners. Notices sprang up on outside walls in every town, promising that our sick and wounded soldiers would be first released. No one I knew volunteered. Exasperated by the poor response, German authorities resorted to another, more ruthless strategy.

The farms in France were small in size and the farmers could not afford the big machines needed at harvest time. Instead, they took turns renting the equipment from a co-op, and then men and threshing machines traveled from farm to farm until the harvest would be completed. My father belonged to such a crew.

One early morning, as the noisy threshing machines separated the grain from its husks in the back of the farmhouse, my father stepped into the woods for a few minutes. A roaring noise coming from the dirt road alerted his attention. German soldiers, jumping out of their trucks, swiftly surrounded the working men and pointed their guns as if ready to shoot. An officer, impeccable in his uniform, stepped in and meticulously inspected each worker. At his command, the guards who followed him grabbed the selected victims and forced them to climb to one of the trucks, where more armed guards shoved them further inside. When it was over, only a few of my father's companions remained. The young and strong had been taken away. My father was powerless and remained hidden behind tall weeds. Stunned and numb, he rejoined the men who had been spared and together they faced the dreadful task of bringing the news to the unfortunate families. The workers so abruptly seized were deported to Germany at once, with no chance of saying goodbye or packing a few belongings. The Germans repeated this horrible practice all over the land to satisfy their huge demand for forced labor. They would arrive unannounced and surround a farm, a factory, or even a movie theater filled with teenagers, and let no one escape. No place was safe.

They also rapidly tightened their grips over farmers by watching them more closely, and tricking them. Disguised in rugged civilian clothes and speaking French fluently, they furtively came out of the woods, imitating the Maquisards and begged farmers for food. A day or so later, the Gestapo would appear, arrest the farmer who had complied, along with his family, confiscate the land and animals and close the farm.

Out of fear, farmers became reluctant to sell food to strangers. Furthermore, obliged to supply the German army with an ever-increasing portion of their crops and dairy products, the farmers had less and less for themselves. The nearby farm that provided us with extra milk and eggs while we lived in the country abruptly refused to give us more than our rations allowed. Cheese became a luxury that my father procured for us by continuing to work part-time at his familiar farm further away. Local butcher shops closed down permanently. A few in the city would open once in a while, but by the time we arrived on our bicycles, no meat remained. We survived on vegetable soups made of potatoes, carrots, leeks and turnips. My father ate the leftovers for breakfast and let us have the hot cereals. For lunch, when in season, my mother cooked wild mushrooms which she collected in the woods. Spending hours in the fields, she dug, cleaned, and trimmed huge quantities of dandelion greens, turning them into endless salads. One late afternoon, our adopted grandmother sent me to buy a few pounds of potatoes from another farm up the hill. The potatoes were small, old and wrinkled, the kind we usually reserved for cattle feed or just threw away. Nevertheless, I was glad to buy them. Walking back home, I spotted a chicken leaving the underbrush across the road. Looking more closely, something small and white caught my attention—an egg! Wasting no time, I ran to pick it up gently, as if holding a treasure. The farmer had seen me, and recouping his chicken, started to walk in my direction. Without hesitation, I poked a hole at the top of the egg and swallowed the thick liquid, then left before the farmer could ask me any question. I returned the next day and the day after, in hope of discovering more eggs. I found none.

Not only did food grow painfully scarce during the German occupation, but so did all sorts of other goods. In our home, we used an oil lamp that we placed above the kitchen table to bring light to the room. Our supply of oil, already terribly low, proved more and more difficult to replenish. We moved around the house in the dark, lighting our lamp only for a short time in the evening while we ate. In winter, when the days shortened, Michel and I took turns doing our homework in front of the tiny open door of the wood-burning stove. The fire inside illuminated our pages and notebooks and kept our fingers warm. After we went to bed, my mother replaced us, taking advantage of the last embers. Sitting on a low chair, leaning toward the flames, she struggled to read the newspaper my father brought back from the city. On extremely cold nights, we kept the stove burning by loading it with more expensive charcoal.

My parents, who both grew up on the farm and worked hard at an early age, were used to hardship, but sometimes the obstacles seemed overwhelming even to them. I remember the day we ran out of wood. I do not know whether my parents lacked the money, or the store lacked the supplies. In any event, we had no more wood to burn. Winter raged outside and the house grew cold. We could not cook dinner and I could not do any homework. My father, who had returned to his factory work in the city when the farmer laid him off in the fall, was late coming home and we worried for him, too. Suddenly my mother stood up, and armed with a hatchet and a hammer, she dashed out of the house saying, "Stay here, I'll be back soon."

We then heard banging. We heard things breaking and crashing—strange noises coming from the empty apartment next door. We heard our mother swearing and badly frightened, we thought she had gone mad. The noise finally calmed down. The door opened and there stood our mother, looking messy and worn out, but with a big load of wood in her arms. "Start the fire," she said simply. We did. Mother had rescued us. The dinner was cooked, and as the room warmed up, we felt happy. Our father, however, was not home yet.

We always feared that our father would be picked up somewhere and sent to a labor camp. We wondered if we would always stay together and worried every day about having enough food to eat. Night had fallen and still there was no sign of our father. We sensed something awful had happened. We lived so far away it would take a long time for anyone to reach us. We kept the fire burning and the pot of soup warm, and we sat waiting. We were so absorbed in our thoughts and feelings that we never heard the sound of footsteps outside. Suddenly, the door opened and there entered my father, alive and well, completely surprised to find us still awake. We looked at him with amazement, and he told us the news: his bicycle had broken down. He had stopped at several shops in the city, but the parts could not be found, and he had walked the entire twelve kilometers, dragging the bicycle and thinking all along, "I cannot travel this distance anymore, especially during the bad weather." Father and bicycle looked broken-spirited.

"We only have one option," he continued. "Move back to the city."

He explained he knew of a distillery located outside the town with some vacant apartments closeby. Confident that he would be hired and possibly earn a little more money, he wanted to spend the next day making all the arrangements. And so it was decided. We stayed up very late that night, talking and preparing, while my mother put more of the wood from the next-door apartment into the stove.

When I woke up the next morning, Father had already left, borrowing my mother's bicycle. We skipped school that day and to occupy ourselves, Michel and I went to check the damage our mother had done the night before.

We pushed open the unlocked door and gasped at the mess of debris on the floor. A kitchen table and four chairs belonging to the landlord had been chopped to pieces. Remnants lay on the floor. The pantry cupboard had lost a couple of shelves. A family with two young children had moved in a few months before but left soon afterward. Surely the landlord had inspected the premises then. What will he say? Should we tell our father? We feared trouble but decided to keep quiet. Little did we know that my father, later on, was going to pay dearly for an evening about which he knew nothing.

As anticipated, my father found a job and rented a two-room row house on the outskirts of Bourges, our old town. *Le Grand Mazières*, as our new place was called, enjoyed electricity. We tried to imagine the thrill of lighting up a whole room by turning a switch. We moved the following weekend. Despite the strict surveillance from the German police, people still circulated within the country, trying to escape the rigors of the war. Our abrupt departure, if noticed, would hardly surprise anyone.

For some unknown reason, I do not remember any of this second move: not the packing and unpacking, nor the trip itself, not even my first impression of our new place. The memories start later. My heart felt sad about leaving the big bright house behind with all the space around it. Most of all, I knew deep inside that we were going back to the war zone. Christmas 1941 had come and gone, that year, without any celebration.

(l-r) My Gandmother, my mother Raymonde Depres, me, Odette, my sister Lucienne and my brother Michel about 1939.

My father at about age twenty in the uniform of the French Army before their defeat in World War II.

Chapter 3

The air felt warm on my face earlier that morning as I walked to school. The sun shone brightly at the moment between the cracks of the wooden door at the entrance of the tunnel. It was early spring 1942 and Europe was in the grip of World War II. Hitler's army had conquered country after country and reached the doorstep of Moscow, where it finally met great resistance. Way south, even the deserts of North Africa, I heard, were under German control. German soldiers occupied my town, too, in France, as I sat in an air raid shelter. I was eleven years old.

A short while before we had been laboring over a math test. The only noise to be heard was that of pens scratching paper and pages being flipped. Then, abruptly, sirens erupted, making us seek shelter immediately. Like trained robots, we stood and left the room. From the hallway we looked for the nearest exit and spilled out into the schoolyard. Already we heard the rumbling sound of heavily loaded planes high over our heads. Teachers across the yard held shelter doors wide opened and rushed us inside.

"*Vite, vite, dépêchons nous!*" (quick, quick, let's hurry) they shouted, gesticulating with their arms.

Air raids were happening everywhere, day and night, disturbing our lives and destroying our cities. Children, tired and scared, played less and less. I remember Claude, the boy next door. As I pointed out how beautiful the sky looked, completely unblemished, and what a pretty day lay ahead, I was startled by his outburst:

"I hate blue skies. I hate beautiful days."

"Why?" I asked in amazement.

"Because that's when the planes come," he grumbled.

Claude was right. The air raids seemed much more frequent in clear weather. Fortunately, our town was not always the target. Squadrons of bombers appeared suddenly and sent us scurrying for safety, while they merely flew over us to other distant missions. The next day's newspaper would invariably inform us which town had been hit and which Allied forces were involved: English, Canadian or American. In time, a man in my neighborhood learned to identify the different motor sounds of the various bombers. We took cover when he yelled "Americans!" as we knew the bombardiers would aim for the factory and miss.

The school's shelter was a long, dark corridor, deep underground. Benches lined both sides of the narrow passage. The deeper we went, the more damp and cold it felt. Blankets were passed around, and we snuggled closer together. Scattered dim lights let us see plainly only the classmate next to us. Outside, muffled sounds caused us to guess at what was happening. After a while, we suspected that the planes had gone.

"It is not for us this time," someone explained.

Still, we did not dare go outside until we heard the long siren signaling danger was gone. Planes were known to drop their bombs anywhere they chose before returning to base.

Air raids could last two or three hours. Ours that day lasted long after lunchtime. Hungry and cramped, we slowly walked back to our classes. Our teachers let us talk and talk until tension was released. The math test was canceled.

Day-time air raids frightened us, but at night they utterly exhausted us. We coped badly with our first one, just a couple months after our arrival to our new place, Le Grand Mazières. Conveniently located midway between the edge of the town and the distillery where my father found a job, this little hamlet seemed the perfect place to live to shorten the long bicycle commute he faced everyday. Nestled alongside a refreshing stream that curved to feed a pond in the back of the building, Le Grand Mazières, with its farm, its trees and open spaces, appealed to young children too, who regarded it as a wonderful playground. How could we have suspected that the small factory barely visible behind tall trees half a kilometer away, and which made only farm equipment before the war, would eventually become the cause of all our fears? But it did. The Germans seized the factory soon after they invaded the country, and transformed it into a war machinery plant instead. The Allied Forces, quickly alerted, started the bombing.

We were sound asleep when, like in a foggy dream, an annoying buzzer that did not stop made me toss and turn until it finally woke me.

"Air raid!" my mind screamed, recognizing the screeching sirens. Reaching for the pile of clothes that I had folded on the floor next to my bed, I started to dress in the dark. I felt my little sister doing the same.

We didn't waste any time talking. My father turned on the light switch and in a dash, we were standing in front of the gas masks hanging on the wall. We each picked our own. Suddenly there was a loud banging on the door and a boy's voice cried: "*Debout, vite! Suivez moi.*"

We rushed outside to meet Claude, who wanted to guide us to the shelter. My mother was the last one out. She slammed the door behind her and said, "*J'ai la boite aux papiers,*" meaning she had not forgotten to take along the tin box containing all our important papers, most especially the ration cards. We kept the box within easy reach on the buffet, a small piece of furniture holding our dishes and food. Claude took the lead and we found ourselves running into the night toward an unknown shelter.

Spring had been wet that year, and the stream flowing by the side of our building had swollen and flooded the part of our path which dipped across a narrow patch of marsh land. Stepping stones were scattered along the way to keep our feet from getting wet. In the darkness, however, we only stumbled against them and fell. Claude, impatiently looking to the sky, yelled, "*Vite, plus vite!*"

We finally reached higher ground, followed a stretch of railroad tracks, crossed a bridge over a canal, and descended into a wide dirt path that was lined with trees. Where was the shelter?

Out of breath and staggering, my mother leaned against a tree and refused to run any longer. My father, with my sister in his arms, joined her. The sirens had stopped and the calmness of the night surprised us. We heard no sound of airplanes. Claude, slowing down himself, broke the silence by pointing out a group of houses taking shape in the distance. "Over there," he told us, "is the shelter."

With renewed strength, we resumed our walk and before long, a huge dark mass appeared on our left. "This is it," Claude announced simply, pushing open two large steel doors.

"The shelter, at last," I exclaimed.

Bright lights blinded us as we entered. A multitude of strangers talked animatedly and welcomed us as we pushed our way into a corner where a few of our neighbors were sitting. "This shelter is an old hangar, protected by sandbags and dirt," we were told.

We had only been in the shelter a short time when a man ran in shouting, "False alert." The planes, apparently, had taken a different direction. We walked back home slowly, hoping to catch a few more hours of sleep before dawn.

It must have been in the early hours of the morning when, once again, the sirens sounded. For the second time, I felt for my clothes on the floor, half-asleep, and prepared to leave. With relief, I heard my mother's weary voice. "Let's stay," she told us. "We can't run anymore, the shelter is too far away. Besides, Grandmère is not strong enough to make another trip."

In a flash, I realized the magnitude of my mother's decision, and for the first time, I pondered the possibility that we might not be alive tomorrow. I was so tired that I fell back to sleep.

The following weekend, my mother took me along to a store near the airport. On the way back, we opted to walk across the farmer's field instead of following the road leading to the semi-hidden factory where they made parts for war machinery. German guards, walking back and forth, constantly patrolled the area. Halfway into the field, sirens screeched, giving us a jolt. Immediately, we saw menacing airplanes flying low. As we ran toward a grove of trees in order to hide underneath, bombs exploded around us. Every detonation made us bend over and shrivel. The noise, the cracking in the air, was deafening, and I clenched my teeth so tightly that my jaw hurt. My mother handed me her leather wallet and said: "Bite on it." Something hard hit my leg and I screamed, "I am hit!"

Just then, a miracle happened. A panel of earth raised itself up in front of us like a door opening, and a rugged voice called: *"Venez ici."* (Come here) We ran wildly to it, tumbled down two or three steps and collapsed at the bottom of a miniature cabin: a farmer's shelter. Three workers already standing there squeezed closer together to give us room. My mother anxiously checked my leg. There was nothing, only scratches from twigs or fallen branches.

The air raid was short but brutal and, I thought, unfair. Innocent young children were killed that day, while all the enemy soldiers survived. When we climbed out of our hole in the ground, an acute smell of burnt chemicals, strong like acid, permeated the air and our nostrils. A thick, heavy, deadly silence enveloped us all. No birds chirping, no insects flying. The field was littered with broken leaves and branches and other debris. As we walked back we noticed the factory stood untouched while a house nearby lay in rubbles. A vehicle passed—an ambulance. We pressed on feverishly. When we entered our courtyard, we met a group of men wearing special armbands on their sleeves. "The Civil Defense volunteer team," my mother explained.

A canal behind our small cluster of buildings normally attracted many townspeople on sunny days and served as a favorite spot for fishermen. On this late afternoon, school children who had been wandering along the banks of the canal when the air raid began sought refuge under trees and bushes. Tragically, stray bombs exploded above them, maiming and killing. The men wearing armbands were desperately trying to reach them, using our yard as a throughway. Stretcher after stretcher passed in front of my kitchen window, as victims were being carried to the vehicles parked up the road. One, then another, completely covered with leaves and branches, made me understand that the victim was no longer alive.

Saddened and outraged, the grown-ups in my neighborhood could not comprehend the horrible errors committed in broad daylight by our allies. We were French, living on French soil. The Germans were the invaders, the enemy that had to be flushed out of France and destroyed. Couldn't the bombardiers be more accurate?

Years have passed since this terrible episode. The war is over. The factory behind our house and the airport just southeast of it were never destroyed, while we buried many more civilians. Our own building eventually crumbled, mostly from age and neglect, but also because of the countless pieces of shrapnel hitting the outside walls and fragmenting the stones. Our window shutters, full of holes burnt through the wood, became useless. Obviously, I survived. I now write about the horrors of the war to ease the pain as memories slowly begin to fade.

Chapter 4

Queuing For Food

The strident noise of an alarm clock ringing next to my ears shook me out of a deep sleep. Five a.m., my eyes registered before my head went plunging back into the pillow. Then I remembered and jumped out of bed: Sunday! "Today is Sunday. My turn to go food shopping!" In no time I dressed myself warmly, added more charcoal to the stove that my parents had kept burning all night long and quietly stepped outside.

The cold air whipped my face, and I pulled the scarf tighter around my cheeks. The courtyard, bathed in moonlight, was full of eerie shadows and dark corners. It frightened me. A few yards away, the tall, bare trees along the deserted canal intimidated me even more. They looked like grim monsters with stretched-out, deformed arms, their bizarre silhouettes reflected in the shimmering water of the canal, a sinister sight. A strong impulse came over me. I wanted to run back inside the safety of my home, but instead, I stood motionless, afraid to take another step, absorbed in the deep silence around me. The houses slept behind shutters closed so tight no light filtered through. Suddenly, I heard a door squeal.

"Odette, Odette, wait for me," someone called.

I recognized my friend Jeannine's voice, and when I saw her emerge all bundled up, with shopping bags in both arms, I had to ask with curiosity: "Where are you going?"

"With you," she answered with aplomb. "Your mom told me last night you were going to the store," she went on, "and I persuaded my parents to let me go, too. Sorry I am late," she added.

"Not at all," I reassured her promptly, astounded and happy all at once to have a companion.

Jeannine lived next door to us and was only ten years old, but so bold and determined, so stubborn, that her parents, I suspect, gave their consent from exhaustion. With my fear fading away, I started to laugh.

"Let's go," I said, and taking the lead, I walked straight across the gloomy railroad tracks, reached the canal and its huge bare trees, and with Jeannine at my side, bravely embarked on a near three-kilometer trek to the nearest market.

Meat, among other food items, had become rare. Some butcher shops had closed their doors permanently, while others used the local newspaper to announce a sporadic arrival of mostly second-grade cuts (discarded from the German army who helped themselves first) and to inform the public on which day and what few hours they intended to stay open.

This created a sort of madness among housewives, who always struggled to find enough food for their families. Getting up in what seemed the middle of the night, they quietly arrived in the darkness and stood in line on the hard pavement, hours before the store opened, in the hope of getting in before the supply ran out.

My mother, too, scrutinized the newspapers and discovered that our familiar butcher shop often opened on Sunday mornings. I, being freed from school on those days, gladly volunteered to replace her. A back injury from years ago made it rather painful for her to stand for a long time. Besides, it felt good for me to be useful. Michel, growing up strong and muscular, risked being sent to a labor camp if spotted and caught by one of the numerous German patrols and my sister Lucienne, still much too young, could not be trusted with any errand. Ironically, my frail, raggedy childish look gave me more freedom to wander in the streets. Jeannine's mother, I presume, thought the same.

It took forty minutes for Jeannine and me to reach the edge of town, walking as fast as we possibly could and without encountering anyone on that stretch of the canal. In town, we noticed the lampposts were not functioning, and the streets would have been pitch-dark without the moon to give us some light. When we arrived at the butcher's shop, we joined a group of women already congregating ahead of us. Clustered together, they were tapping their feet on the sidewalk to keep them warm. One hour passed, then another. The line grew longer as more people arrived. To occupy themselves, some women chatted, mostly complaining about the weather.

"When will this winter end?" one of them asked.

"I am out of charcoal at home and I walked from store to store yesterday only to find them all empty," another added.

Then everyone agreed on how difficult it had become to plan a meal. By then, Jeannine and I shivered under our coats and our feet, numbed by the cold, hurt when we moved them. Standing on one leg, then another, we leaned against each other for more support and stopped talking to save our energy. We wished the store would open soon. When it finally did, the first wave of customers pushed us inside a big, unheated room where we squeezed to let more people in. Small and surrounded by taller persons who blocked my view, I could not see the amount of meat available, and I cringed when I heard someone ask for a big quantity of soup bones and liver, two items my mother insisted I buy. They were economical and not rationed.

What if the supply runs out before my turn? I kept worrying. To my relief, Jeannine and I soon stood up front, ready to be helped. The butcher and his son worked diligently, cutting through big pieces of meat with sharp knives, their hands red and swollen from pushing away chunks of ice that covered the counter. Once in a while, they warmed their fingers against a small electric heater placed in front of them.

"Next," the butcher called.

Readily I gave him my ration card coupons, which we had saved for a month. I asked him for stew meat, a couple of thin steaks, some other kind of meat called *pot-au-feu* which my mother simmered in a stock pot along with all sorts of vegetables, extra soup bones and a few slices of liver. The butcher complied. Feeling extremely happy, I joined Jeannine already waiting for me, a smile on her face, and both of us crossed the street to the bakery to buy our ration of bread for the next two days, then went on to another grocery store for fruits and vegetables among other items. There, we learned hand soap was being sold several streets farther away. Taking a chance, we searched for the place, only to arrive too late —the supply had run out. A bit discouraged and very tired, we slowly retraced our steps, carrying heavy shopping bags in each hand while the rough cobblestones of the street made the pain in our legs more acute.

Opting for a narrow little passageway, we stumbled into the back of a huge, dark building that I knew as *St. Pierre* or St. Peter's church. Sounds of music were filtering through a door left ajar. Filled with curiosity, I pulled Jeannine inside, and noting a group of people occupying the first few rows, we furtively sneaked to the back, hoping to be unnoticed. There we stood behind empty benches, afraid to sit down, feeling strange and out of place with our grocery bags lined up in front of us on the hard floor. The church felt damp, and cold drafts hit us from everywhere. Nevertheless, with our eyes riveted to the front of the church, we tried very hard to comprehend the religious service in progress. Our families did not practice any religion and only on special occasions would someone in the neighborhood attend a church ceremony.

"We live too far away," became the favorite excuse for everyone.

The organ music, subdued at first, now filled the church with vibrant sounds which made us feel warm inside and lifted our spirits. For an instant, I was forgetting the war, the soldiers, the bombs, and my hungry stomach. In a flash I was transported back to my grandmother's village where life seemed safer and uncomplicated. Grandmother went to church and thought of Sunday as her biggest social event of the week. On that day most of the villagers, young and old, gathered on the square, greeting each other cheerfully and sharing some family news. The older people, especially, bubbled with enthusiasm and laughter. Only the church bells, which rang softly at first but then more imperatively, would temper the exuberance of its parishioners by inviting them inside. My favorite seat in Grandmother's church had always awaited me: a niche in the wall not far from a long stained-glass window that I read like a storybook, with its beautiful figures dancing in the morning sun. The fragrance of incense, the sight of lighted candles, the old people slowly leaving the church and resuming their chatting again, were only cherished memories coming alive magically in my mind as I listened to the choir of St. Peter's Church. I longed for my grandmother's Sunday dinners. In my imagination, I could even smell the aroma of meat roasting in a thick heavy pan, and hear the crackling sound of wood burning in the kitchen stove. But someone was shaking me: "Odette, let's go," Jeannine kept repeating. "We have rested enough and it's getting late." So we left reluctantly. We knew our mothers waited for us to cook their our own Sunday dinners.

Jeannine and I made many more similar trips during the following months and, like a ritual, we continued to stop and rest at St. Peter's church if only for a few minutes.

Chapter 5

The Day Our Ration Cards Vanished

The cold days of winter slowly faded away. Spring 1943 came, bringing with it the local flood. Every year at this time our calm little stream called La Rampenne transformed itself into a swollen torrent that inundated all the gardens stretching along its low borders. It also flooded our walking path that dipped across a narrow patch of swampy land before reaching the railroad tracks on higher grounds, our common route to town, school or work.

Every year, neighbors piled stepping-stones strategically, but no matter how hard they tried, the water overran the stones, inevitably making them slippery and dangerous. Still, some working teenage boys, eager to show off their skill with their bicycles over their heads, hopped from stone to stone, laughing and enjoying their precariously balanced bravado.

For many, though, the wooden bridge at the entrance of our courtyard proved to be the biggest challenge. It was narrow with no guardrails and partly decayed; the planks, thin and worn out at places, let a few bolts stick out to trip unwary feet. Cracks between the middle boards were large enough to trap a bicycle wheel and throw the driver down. A man attempting to cross the bridge riding on his bicycle one late dark night lost his balance and tumbled down into the icy water. Children, too, occasionally fell overboard when playing or running too fast across the bumpy structure. Luckily, everyone was plucked out promptly and no one suffered serious damage, only humiliation.

My turn was just about to come. I had overslept one Sunday morning and tried to hurry. Jeannine's familiar knock on the door a few minutes earlier gave me the signal she was ready and waiting for me to start our regular food-shopping endeavor.

Grabbing a couple of tote bags, the ration cards, and the money my mother had neatly arranged on the kitchen table the night before, I rushed outside. When I saw Jeannine on the railroad tracks, I ran to join her. I'd barely entered the bridge when my foot tripped on something hard and I was thrown tumbling across the bridge. My fingers found a crack in the wood at the last minute and held on, while my legs wound tight around the edge of a board. I was in a precarious position, nearly upside down, and knew I couldn't hold on much longer. "Jeannine!" I yelled.

Jeannine had heard the noise, and guessing the worst, rushed to help. She found me quickly, and in the near darkness proceeded to grab on whatever she could—clothes, arms or legs. At times, I thought we were both going to catapult into the raging water, and yet, we were laughing. Finally, I managed to roll back onto the bridge. Feeling exhausted and more embarrassed than hurt, except for the scratches on my fingers, I slowly gathered my belongings that had scattered around: a tote bag here, some money there, the ration cards... Where were the rations cards?

"What happened to them?" I shouted again and again with panic in my voice.

Jeannine and I crawled on our hands and knees all along the bridge searching for the ration cards, to no avail. Daybreak was filtering through, and as I glanced at the stream, I noticed how strong the current was and how fast it carried everything away.

"If my ration cards fell overboard, we'll never find them," I moaned. "What can we buy without ration coupons?" I wondered. "Everything we eat is rationed: milk, bread, meat, cheese, eggs, butter, jam, among much other food; and those rations are extremely small, even inadequate, but still they keep us alive. Without them, we'll probably starve!"

The farm up the hill where we bought our daily allowance of milk—a small cup per child —was so closely watched by Germans dressed in civilian clothes and speaking French that the farmer would never risk his livelihood by selling us milk without coupons. Distribution time was punctual and lasted exactly one hour every late afternoon. Then the gate closed, all the doors locked, and the Germans departed with the leftover milk and whatever other dairy product they needed. The farmer was a prisoner in his own farm.

I was deep in these somber thoughts when I heard Jeannine's voice coming to me like through a fog. "Wake Michel up. Maybe he can help," she was saying.

"Good idea," I replied, shaking my gloomy spirit away. Then, realizing how much precious time Jeannine had already lost because of me, I added:

"Go on without me. You might still be able to get some meat at the butcher's shop if you hurry."

Jeannine nodded and left. As I watched her disappear, I felt vaguely that our adventurous shopping trips together were coming to an end.

Back in the house, I gently shook Michel out of his sleep. Opening his eyes halfway, he kept asking, "What? What happened?"

I told him my story. "The ration cards . . . they're gone. They fell into the creek. I can't go shopping. Come, help me find them."

Finally, Michel understood, dressed quickly, and then followed me. In the daylight, the bridge looked clean of any debris. My brother gazed around. Then without hesitation, he took his shoes off and went wading into the icy cold water at the edge of the stream, checking every clump of reeds in the hope our ration cards might have drifted there. He kept on searching until his hands became red and swollen, but he found nothing.

Some noise around the chicken enclosure alerted me that my father, a farmer at heart, was up already doing his chores. My parents, imitating the neighbors, were trying to enlarge our food supply by raising rabbits, chickens and even a few ducks. We caught up with my father as he was feeding the animals. One look at us and he knew immediately that something was wrong. We explained quickly.

My father was a quiet man who never lost his temper. He listened to me patiently. When I stopped talking, he said calmly: "I know a farmer who would help us if only we could safely go to his farm."

"Who?" Michel and I exploded. "Which farm?" we asked, regaining some hope.

"The farm where I worked when we lived in the countryside the first year of the war," my father continued. "Remember? The farmer was a kind man and always gave us extra food. Unfortunately, the roads are heavily patrolled these days and the Germans arrest anyone caught buying food in the black market."

Suddenly, he looked at my brother. "No, no, you cannot go, not you," he exclaimed, guessing what Michel was about to suggest. "You are strong for your young age and the Germans would not hesitate to send you to a labor camp if they ever caught you. We would never see you again."

My father, shaken at the thought of what could happen to Michel at the hands of the German soldiers, stopped the conversation. I watched him walk slowly into the garden shed, slightly bent over and heard him lament: "How will we survive without ration cards?"

Chapter 6

The Baby Carriage

The painful sight of my father looking defeated that day worried me. I followed him silently to the shed where I stood at the entrance wondering what to do next. He was walking back and forth, inspecting his tools one by one, obviously distraught. Suddenly, something else caught my attention. There, in a corner collecting dust stood the answer to our problems. Immediately, a grand idea sprang into my head and I blurted out: "Papa, I know! I know what to do! We'll have food tonight!" I kept shouting with excitement. "Look, Papa, behind the wheelbarrow. Do you see it?"

I crossed the shed as fast as I could and pulled a big dark object out of the corner. Watching me, my father exclaimed: "What? A baby carriage? Are you well? What can you do with a baby carriage?"

"Everything," I assured him. Michel, who had been listening to the whole dialogue, looked just as puzzled as my father. I had to explain. "Haven't you noticed how easily young children go through a German barricade? The guards ignore them completely. They stop the adults by yelling a *Halt* order and demand *papeers*, but I've seen little girls push their doll carriages right by the German soldiers without being checked. I'm certain I can go from farm to farm, using the back-roads in the countryside, without bringing attention from the Germans patrolling the area. They'll think I'm just a little girl taking a walk in her neighborhood, and they'll disregard me" I continued, trying to plead my case the best I could.

"It might work," said Michel, supporting me. My father was more doubtful. "You can't walk that far," he said. "Besides, this small size carriage is still too big to pretend to be a toy and you don't play with dolls anymore."

My father was half-right. True, this carriage had been roomy enough at one time to hold either my brother, sister or myself, when we were babies, but a lot of use had left it rather unpretentious and worn looking. It was exactly the kind of discarded household item that parents let their children play with. No, I didn't play with dolls anymore. "No time and too many chores," I grumbled.

I only had one doll, anyway. But what a special and wonderful doll it was! Tall as a toddler, it walked and turned its head from side to side when I guided it gently by the hand. It looked resplendent in its bright pink outfit, curly blond hair, and sparkling blue eyes. As I constantly feared that my siblings would break it, I tucked it away in my mother's armoire, when I didn't play with it. As always, thinking about the doll made me remember how I'd acquired it.

I was impatiently waiting for Christmas, that year, just before my seventh birthday. The stores displayed enticing toys in their windows. On that particular day, the older sister of a little girl I played with, decided to tell us both the truth about Santa Claus, or Père Noël as we called him. I listened to her with disbelief, and feeling something crumble within me, I rushed to my mother. I expected her to discredit what I'd just heard. To my dismay, she not only reinforced the girl's story, but went on to explain that because I finally knew the truth about Santa Claus, I certainly would understand why there would be no more presents for me on Christmas day. My father didn't make enough money and there were two other children to think of . . . and so on.

I was crushed. I stopped listening and when Christmas morning finally arrived, I refused to get up. I was certain that I would find only oranges and chocolate candies in my shoes, the way my father always found carrots and potatoes. With a chuckle, he would shrug off a fake disappointment and claimed he had been bad and Santa knew it. Actually, adults never received presents from Santa Claus on Christmas. The day was reserved for young children. Apparently, parents took their turn on New Year's eve with Bonhomme Janvier.

I was pondering all those thoughts lying in bed that Christmas day, when cries of excitement forced me to pick up my head. "Odette, come and see!" I heard Michel shout. "You have a doll, a big doll!"

"What?" I cried, "It can't be," I told myself, remembering my mother's words but still curious enough to get out of bed. Then I saw it. Propped up against the wall, and halfway out of its box, stood the most beautiful doll I had ever imagined. "Oh," I exclaimed, dropping next to her and touching her softly, "She's so pretty. Is she mine, really?"

My mother was smiling and helped me to get her completely out of the box. She bent over to whisper a secret. "Yes, she's yours. Santa thought you deserved it."

I was overwhelmed by the moment. A tea service and other practical items, like gloves and socks, completed my Christmas but my eyes kept turning to the doll. I don't know what Santa brought to my brother and sister that year. My father's boots showed the traditional array of vegetables and fruits with some candies mixed in. That was my last and best Christmas. The following ones were swept away by the war.

Suddenly, a vibrant *"Voilà!"* snapped me out of my melancholic mood. While I was so deeply reminiscing, my father had quietly dusted the webs out of the baby carriage. Michel, who had astutely figured out my plan, handed me my special doll. Together, we cushioned it in the carriage on layers of folded blankets underneath which I could hide eggs, cheese and butter. My father pointed out the double-bottom he had discovered where bottles of milk could fit nicely. It all looked perfect and I was anxious to start my trip. Early-risers were already tending their gardens. Noise inside the house warned me that my mother was up also.

"You'd better hurry," my father said, "Your mother might be hard to convince to let you go so far."

My father was right, so I left quickly while he went in to explain. Michel accompanied me across the dreary bridge, the railroad tracks and up to the lock where we separated. Because of my late start, I decided not to go to my father's favorite farm, as I would have to cross the part of town where Jeannine and other shoppers might meet me and ask curious questions. Nobody should know about my illegal and dangerous venture. Instead, I turned into the opposite direction, going through unfamiliar territory, along a deserted canal, hoping to discover a small country road that could lead me to several farms.

I waved happily to Michel who was still watching me. I felt brave and daring as I stepped forward on the narrow path, pushing a baby carriage in front of me with my doll inside who, I think, was smiling. I was twelve years old.

Chapter 7

My First Day on the Black Market

The canal stretched in front of me like a long shiny ribbon, unfurling between tall trees that made a canopy over my head. Behind the trees, large bushes reinforced the sense of enclosure, while farther away at the horizon the canal disappeared, engulfed by a mass of dark foliage. I could not see beyond and it worried me.

"Soldiers might be hidden and waiting for me," I thought aloud. "German patrols could be setting traps to catch wandering people."

I slowed down and tried to listen for telltale signs of military presence, like harsh commands, heavy footing or even the clanking of guns. I heard nothing but the constant squeaking noise of my own baby carriage. In my haste and excitement, I had forgotten to oil the wheels.

"Anyone can not only see me, but hear me as well," I told myself angrily. My eyes kept searching the banks of the canal, hoping to find a fisherman who could inform me of what stood ahead, but I found none. I was all alone.

This segment of the canal was certainly new to me, and it frightened me. How I missed walking with Jeannine on our more familiar path toward town where every tree, every shadow had become a friend. To occupy myself, I started to focus on the puddles of light the sun made on the water when it filtered through the branches. They flickered, danced, and brightened the muddy water. I heard a bird singing, then another, and my mood slowly changed. Picking up speed, I soon reached my "horizon," this special spot where everything, sky, canal and trees, blended into darkness, and out of complete surprise I joyfully cried: "A lock!"

I recognized instantly the gray and wet walls of concrete that hold the water after it tumbles down when the lock empties itself. I knew all about locks, for I had spent hours studying the one next to our house.

It all starts when the barge announces itself by blowing its horn repeatedly. This prompts the lockkeeper to rush out and determine in which direction the barge is traveling. Then, he either fills or empties the lock, adjusting the water level to accommodate the incoming barge. Gates open and close, water cascades in or out and splashes along the walls before spilling into the small harbor. The barge glides in smoothly, gets raised or lowered, and then passes through on its way to the next lock. I watched, entirely fascinated. Entire families lived on those barges, earning their livelihood by transporting goods (bricks, lumber, among other material) from town to town. My own grandmother grew up on such a barge and spent most of her childhood crisscrossing the region. In the wintertime when the canal froze, her parents anchored their boat safely on the banks of the canal near a village called Villefranche-sur-Cher and waited for spring. During one of those cold spells, my grandmother met a handsome farmer and married him, thus giving up forever the "boat life" to settle permanently in this lovely village which I visited so often before the war.

While reminiscing about my grandmother and her village, I had climbed the ramp that led to the bridge above. It was deserted and no sound came out of the lockkeeper's house. The path on my left disappeared in the middle of an empty field, but to my right farther away, a tall building caught my attention. "The distillery," I shouted with a slight disappointment.

I could not believe it. I had walked so long and still I was just a mere kilometer away from my house, close to my father's place of work. My brother and I sometimes ran to the distillery to see the workers. We cut across a quarry and went down an embankment. It seemed so much shorter. A bit dismayed, I went back down to the towpath, looking for the far-away second lock.

As I walked, the canal became more open with fewer bushes to obstruct the view or the sunlight. Some gardens appeared here and there in the low clearing, and I suddenly spotted a gardener filling up a watering can from the canal.

"*Monsieur! Monsieur!*" I called out, happy to see another person.

The man had heard me and was trying hard to recognize me.

"Little girl," he asked with raised eyebrows, "What are you doing here?"

I mumbled something like "taking a walk," remembering my father's admonition: "Don't talk to anyone. Don't attract attention," which he had repeated over and over.

But then, I took a wild chance and asked the gardener bluntly: "How far is the nearest village?" pointing my finger in the direction I wanted to go.

He looked at me a little longer, then answered: "You just passed Germigny." (I knew that!) "At the next lock, take the road on your left. It is safe," he added, nodding his head affirmatively.

I left him, waving *au-revoir*, and thanked him for the information. His directions were correct. At the next lock, I found a road winding through small hills and narrow valleys. It seemed safe enough with no one in sight, but no farm either. I started to wonder where it would lead me, when abruptly around a turn, a village appeared.

 First, I saw the church sitting straight up at the edge of the road. Then I came to a cluster of small homes. I had barely entered the community when a cacophony of barnyard voices came from the left side of the road. I looked, and there across a ditch, I saw the liveliest, most elaborate chicken coop I had ever imagined. It began with a shed at the back of a large covered enclosure where reddish, small-size chickens roamed around freely. Then came a long screened corridor full of rabbit cages lined up against the wall and more chickens going back and forth. Finally, everything—corridor, chickens and even some rabbits—all emerged into an even larger, brighter courtyard already filled with other kind of birds happily scratching the ground everywhere. So much room, so many sounds! The roosters especially could be heard above all others with their loud cockadoodledoos.

What a delightful food factory, I thought. Where is the entrance?

I followed the road downhill and around the turn, then discovered the path that led to a quaint little house tucked neatly between a vegetable garden and a small courtyard.

"This has to be the place," I told myself.

An elderly woman answered my knock on the door and asked what I wanted. It was my first try so it took a long explanation. "I saw your chickens," I started to say, "and we lost our ration cards, and we don't have much to eat and I would like to buy some eggs . . ." I showed my money. I was practically begging a stranger to sell me some eggs.

The lady looked at me more curiously, then assuring herself that I was really alone and not bluffing, pushed the door wide open and said simply, "*Entre,*" inviting me inside.

Once inside the room, she introduced me to her sister, another elderly lady hovering over a hot stove. "Pancakes," the woman explained when I stood next to her. "Potato pancakes," she repeated, taking some more batter from a big bowl and dropping it into a large flat pan. The three of us stood around the stove and watched the patties get brown on both sides. Then the lady-cook piled them up on a platter while her sister proceeded to set the table. I counted three plates.

"Sit here," she insisted, and brought me a chair.

I gladly accepted. We chatted, ate and drank weak coffee. Those ladies seemed delighted to have a visitor. They bombarded me with questions: "Do you see a lot of German soldiers in your town? Did you meet any on your way this morning? You must be hungry, have another pancake," they offered.

Their house felt good and pleasant, and I wished I did not have to go anywhere else. I lingered as long as I could. A basket appeared on the table with six fresh eggs inside for me, "to take home," the first lady explained, reminding me of the reason why I had stopped at their house. I left these ladies reluctantly, but planned to come back on a future trip.

Back on the road and outside the village, I looked out for the farms my new friends had recommended to me. I needed milk, cheese and butter, basic food items that proved very hard to obtain, as I found out.

Most farmers were reticent, even suspicious. They furtively wrapped a soft cheese or a chunk of butter, handed it to me in exchange for my money and quickly sent me on my way, barely saying a few words. Others, somewhat more talkative, apologized for having nothing to sell. They blamed the German authorities who already had appropriated for themselves all the farmers' goods.

I had to go deeper and deeper into the countryside in order to fill up the hidden bottom of my baby carriage. I had left the main highway and wandered on a dirt road that cut across large fields. I was looking for one more farm. One finally appeared in the distance. I aimed for it.

This farm stood away from the road at the end of a long driveway. I was halfway there when something startled me—it was silent, unusually and profoundly silent! Farms in France are noisy havens, with chickens, ducks and other fowl running freely around the yard and chirping endlessly as they scratch for food at the edge of the heap of manure. Other sounds join the chorus from the depth of their barn: goats, sheep, cows, and even whole families of piglets. Then the farmer himself may be heard shouting at his horses while he plows the land.

But this farm had no sound. It looked empty. Yet, equipment and other strewn items were all about: a pitchfork by the barn, the farmer's wagon at the entrance of the yard, a worker's bicycle against the wall. And the unmistakable smell of fresh manure that permeated the air, affirmed me that I had, indeed, arrived at a farm. Suddenly, I sensed someone watching me. Did the curtains just move? Something was wrong, terribly wrong. I froze.

By some involuntary reflex, I picked up my doll and held her tight for a few seconds, straightening her dress. Then I placed her back in the carriage in a sitting position. From far away, I am sure she looked like a real baby girl. I bent down to pick some wild flowers, trying to keep calm, then turned around and slowly headed back to the road. All along I feared somebody would catch up with me.

Another farm stood on my right nearly straight across from the one I had just visited. This one was alive, and people were signaling to me from their doorstep. "Who are you? What are you doing here? We watched you going to the farm over there. Are you a friend of their children?" Question after question was being thrown at me.

Before I could answer, they went on: "The Gestapo is inside. They came in yesterday, arrested the whole family and took the animals away, too. A man rode in on his bicycle very early this morning. The soldiers grabbed him before he had a chance to turn back and we don't know what has happened to him since. That's his bike against the wall. You're lucky you managed to get away."

"Why did the Gestapo arrest them?" I asked, feeling extremely threatened.

"Most every night we see strangers cut across their yard and disappear into the woods over there," the man explained, pointing to a clump of trees in the distance. "We suspect they are Maquisards, and the farmer probably gave them food and shelter. Now the Gestapo is inside the house, waiting for anyone to drop in and we don't know how to warn those young people."

The man's wife, who had been studying me quietly, became curious. "You are not familiar to me. Where do you live? What is your name?"

"I come from Bourges," I answered. "We lost our ration cards and I am walking from farm to farm trying to buy food." I showed her what I had collected already.

The woman looked bewildered: "You came from that far?" she questioned again. Suddenly she realized the danger I was putting them in and screamed with horror in her voice: "You can't stay here. The Gestapo is next door. If they catch you buying food from us, they will arrest us too. Please go. Leave immediately. Take the trail behind the garden wall. Hurry!"

The woman was right, so I left. I walked straight across her yard, went behind the barn and the garden wall, away from both farms. I heard footsteps running after me—her husband. He was calling and waving something at me at the same time.

"Wait! I have a *casse-croûte* for you," he said when he reached me, and handed me a bundle of food hastily wrapped in a newspaper. "You must be hungry," he added. "You are a long way from home."

I looked and saw apples, bread and cheese. I was still thanking him when he interrupted me. "Forgive my wife," he said. "We already lost a few friends to the Gestapo and she is certain we are going to be next." Then, pointing to the field below, he added, "This is a good trail. Follow it to the end. It used to be a short cut to my favorite fishing spot on the canal when I was a boy. Look for the bridge. Go under it and after the first lock, you should recognize your way. *Au revoir.*"

On this we parted, each going in opposite directions. The trail proved very difficult. It was too narrow for my baby carriage, and the wheels stumbled over stones, roots and thick weeds. I pulled and pushed, fell and scratched my knees, but finally landed on the canal towpath, where I quickly sat down under the shade of a tree to catch my breath. The bridge mentioned by the farmer stood only a few yards away. I grabbed an apple from my carriage, and I had barely taken a second bite when I heard terrifying sounds: a truck that came to a screechy halt, harsh words thrown into the air and boots hitting the pavement. To my horror, helmets and gun barrels rose above the safety rail. Germans! A German patrol suddenly crowded the bridge I was about to walk under in order to get home. As I sat there, partially stunned, wondering what to do next, a soft greeting came to me: "*Bonjour,*" it said. I glanced around and saw no one.

"*Bonjour,*" the voice said again. Looking closer to the ground, I discovered a large hat and then, underneath it, a face with two big brown eyes laughing at me.

"Who are you? What are you doing here?" I exclaimed, startled to find someone hidden in the tall grass.

"My name is Pierre," the voice answered, "and I am fishing. Do you have another apple?"

"Of course," I said, astonished to find a little boy but, puzzled, I had to ask: "Haven't you seen the Germans on the bridge? I think they have a bird's-eye view of you from their high point. Aren't you afraid?"

"No," Pierre answered. "My big brother tells me they don't bother small children. Besides, I promised my mother a fish for tonight's dinner. I live in the village. I have never seen you before. Where do you live?"

I was ready to tell him I lived much farther away when I heard him yell: "Oh, look! I have one." Something, indeed, was dangling at the end of his line, and reeling the wiggly beast closer, he yelled: "Quick, hand me the bucket, please."

I complied swiftly and in a matter of minutes, we were both watching a fat, silvery fish swimming in circles in a bucket half-filled with water. "A carp," Pierre announced proudly, "a big one."

"A huge one," I echoed. Excited about his catch and eager to go home, Pierre gathered his fishing gear.

"One fish is enough," he stated.

He looked younger and shorter than me, but he was so much more muscular. His large hat was tossed slightly back and he held his fishing pole over his shoulder in a debonair fashion. All in all, Pierre looked picturesque and full of self confidence. Suddenly, he turned toward me and with a raised pointed finger and a frown crossing his forehead, he exclaimed: "Oh, I remember what I wanted to warn you about. Your toy makes too much noise. I heard you coming down the path long before I could see you. The guards up on the bridge might not bother you when you go by them, as I am sure they have checked us out already, but you might attract other guards' attention elsewhere."

The noise that had annoyed him was the continuous irritating squeak of my wheels. "I know," I said, moving the carriage back and forth to show him where the noise came from. "There is nothing I can do about it until I get home," I explained.

"Oh yes there is. Follow me." Grabbing what he called my toy, he pulled it backward to a wooden deck at the edge of the canal where a ramp sliding into the water seemed to invite children for a swim. Then I watched him plunge my carriage halfway into the water.

All at once I visualized my doll flipping over, along with the food so well camouflaged, so I ran to stop him and yelled: "What are you doing? Are you crazy? Stop, you are spilling my things!"

Furiously, I helped him retrieve the carriage and together we set it back dripping wet on the towpath. Nothing had fallen out. "Try it now and listen," Pierre said casually.

I did and the wheels going forward or backward did not screech any more. "A miracle," I exclaimed.

"No, a trick," retorted Pierre, "a trick I learned from my older brother who tried it once on his squeaky bike when he crossed the woods one night and did not want to be heard."

What was Pierre's older brother doing in the woods at night? I wondered, but did not ask any further questions.

"It only works for a short time," Pierre continued on, commenting on this ingenious trick. "You will have to dry the wheels thoroughly as soon as you get home and oil them well or they will rust."

We had arrived at the edge of the clearing, just before the bridge, and stood under the cover of our last tree when Pierre came up with an idea: "Let me go first. I will distract the guards with my fish, and when you hear my voice, start going under the overpass and maybe you'll have the time to reach the big bushes on the other side before they realize you are not with me."

And so we did. I watched him climb the steps up to the road above. I heard him speak. Could Pierre speak German, too? I wondered. I saw the helmets get closer together and bend downward. I made a dash for the bridge and beyond, walking as fast as I could. I looked back only when I reached a big bush and felt safe. Far in the distance, where the road curved to enter the village, I faintly saw the contour of a large brown hat and the end of a fishing pole moving along behind small hedges. Pierre had made it through.

As for me, the rest of the journey remained unbelievably smooth— no more soldiers, guards or Gestapo. To shake the monotony, at the lock where the distillery stood close by, I switched to the more open path of the railroad tracks, and left the lonely canal behind. (Pierre had encouraged me to be bold.)

The buildings looked deserted on this late Sunday afternoon. Even the gardeners had gone home already, but the more familiar sights renewed my spirit.

With no large trees to obscure my path, I saw my house come into view as soon as I reached the top of the hill. My mother was standing in the doorway, her eyes riveted on the canal, waiting for me. I waved frantically to get her attention. As she finally recognized me walking down the railroad tracks, she yelled a loud *"La voilà!"* to all who could hear her, and ran to meet me.

Later, while we sat around the kitchen table savoring a thick potato omelet, debating and recounting the events of the day, I felt so proud to have been useful to my family one more time. But it had been a long and trying day for me, and suddenly I felt very tired. I curled up my arms on the table, rested my head on them and fell asleep under a cloud of happy chatter.

Many trips followed that first one. I developed several routes and discovered numerous paths crisscrossing the countryside. I tried to see Pierre again, but had no luck. He and his family simply vanished.

Chapter 8

My Father is Taken Away

One month passed. My weekly (sometimes-bi-weekly) food-shopping trips in the countryside were developing into a smooth routine. One day, as I was returning from one of those, I wondered why my mother was not watching for me from our doorstep, as she usually did each time. I had left a little earlier on this Thursday morning (my day off from school), and perhaps she did not expect me home so soon. I felt eager to surprise her.

But the moment I stepped inside my house I knew something terribly wrong had happened. It was early afternoon and the dishes from lunch still lingered on the table, uncleaned, with food left on the plates. Broken chunks of bread, half eaten, rested next to each plate and my father's drinking glass filled with mother's water-diluted wine had barely been touched. No one in my family ever left the table without eating every bite of food served on his plate. Bread, especially, was never to be wasted. We allowed the chicken to come on our kitchen floor after every meal to scrape the crumbs we cleared off the table. Something horrible had forced my family to interrupt their meal. What could have happened to them? I asked myself as I looked over the disarray in the room: my father's chair tipped over, some of my mother's clothes strewn upon the floor, one of my sister's shoes by the bedroom door.

"Mom, Dad, where are you?" I yelled, with panic in my voice. A moan answered me, coming from the alcove behind the wood-burning stove. I ran to it and discovered Grand-mère. Slumped in a chair, she appeared extremely small and frail. "Grand-mère!" I exclaimed, "Are you hurt? What happened here?"

Getting no response, I searched her for visible wounds but found none. Pulling her up gently to make her sit straight against the back of the chair, I noticed how pale she looked in her long black dress. Her eyes followed my movements but stayed blank and distant. All along, I kept on talking to her. "Grand-mère, don't you know me anymore? Please answer me."

Grabbing a towel which I dipped in a bucket full of cool water from the well, I proceeded to pat her forehead and tap her cheeks here and there.

"Wake up, Grand-mère!" I repeated.

After a while, I saw a spark of recognition in her eyes and a few minutes later she muttered: "They . . . they took your father away."

"Who, Grandmère? Who took my father away?" I exclaimed, shaking her a little to keep her talking.

"The Germans . . . the German soldiers with the French police," she went on, picking up some strength in her voice.

"What?" I exploded in disbelief, "What was their reason?"

It took some time, but as she gradually came back to life, she slowly unfolded the story.

"Remember the night your mother burned the furniture from the apartment next to ours, when we lived in the countryside?"

"Of course," I nodded.

"Well," Grand-mère continued, "the landlord filed a complaint and the police have been looking for us ever since."

"How did they find us?" I interrupted angrily.

The answer came to me right away, in a flash. A few days before, my mother had gone to the government office to renew the ration cards we had lost months ago. The clerk had insisted, of course, on seeing her identity card among other papers and the police, under the control of German authorities, checked every record. That's how they found us. So simple and so maddening, I thought.

Meanwhile, Grand-mère was still talking. "You see," she mumbled, "at first your father could not understand why he was being arrested. He struggled, shouting all along that he never destroyed anyone's property. He kept telling them they were mistaken." Grand-mère rested a few seconds, then added: "That's when your mother intervened. She explained to him how she and she alone, on a cold winter night, broke into the apartment next door in search of wood to burn in our stove so we could keep warm and she could cook our dinner. When the police heard your mother's confession, they grabbed her, also, ignoring the pleas and offers from your father to repay the landlord for the damages."

Grand-mère was out of breath. I gave her a glass of water and then I asked, apprehensive of the answer, my heart sinking at the thought of my brother being sent to a forced-labor camp, "And Michel, did they take him too?"

"No," Grand-mère responded, in a more cheerful voice. "Your brother had a project going on somewhere. He ate quickly and left early, long before we heard the German trucks arriving in the yard."

A quick glance at the table made me realize that my brother's plate was, in fact, empty. Grand-mère was talking again. "Lucienne escaped through the bedroom window. I do not know where she went."

Sitting on my knees by her side, my head on her lap, I felt a sense of hopelessness. She kept lamenting. "How are we going to live now that your father is gone? How are we going to pay the rent? You are still too young to get a job and we have no place else to go. Who can help us?"

"I don't know, Grand-mère, I don't know," I repeated again and again. A few minutes later, Michel returned from a friend's house and found us huddled together. We had to relive the whole horrible story for him. Stunned at first, he stayed motionless, showing no expression. Except for anger, my brother knew how to hide his emotions under a cover of toughness. Fortunately for us, catastrophes did not hold him down long. His fighting spirit and fast thinking went to work promptly. Already he had developed a plan: we would all be going to Villefranche-sur-Cher to stay with our grandparents.

"How?" I exclaimed, knowing the local trains ran irregularly, constantly delayed by air raids, and sometimes stranded overnight in desolate areas where the German patrols checked everyone's papers. It would not be safe for my strong and healthy brother. "They'll take you, too," I shouted, "and send you to their forced-labor camp. Besides," I continued, "our grandparents are too old and too poor to take care of all of us for a long time."

"True," Michel answered calmly, but then stated: "They would only have to care for Lucienne. Haven't you noticed how some of their friends have grown fond of both of us over the years, especially the ones who have no children any more? They always invite us to their homes for a few days' vacation. I am sure they would delight in having us permanently."

After a short pause he continued. "You and I will ride our bicycles along the canal. It goes straight to the village. We'll need food and blankets in case we have to rest or even sleep overnight under the trees."

My brother thrived in adversity. The bigger the challenge, the sharper his thinking. A quick search around the house told us we had approximately three days of food supplies counting what I had in my baby carriage, and enough money to spare for two train tickets for Grand-mère and Lucienne. Both were either too young or too old to be bothered by German patrols, we hoped.

Lucienne? Where was she? I sprang to my feet and went looking for her. Walking in the yard, I looked at all the windows. Obviously the neighbors had seen the German police enter my house and arrest my parents, but even though curious and baffled, they were still too wary to approach us for fear that the Germans had not all gone away. Even Michel had decided to sleep away from the house for the next few days, as he was certain the soldiers would come back to pick him up.

"We are not Jewish," I had reminded him, referring to the sneaky tactics of the German police breaking into the Jewish homes in the dead of night to seize entire families while they slept. Jewish people were disappearing in great numbers and nobody knew what was becoming of them. Two of my classmates stopped showing up at school with no explanation, and when our teacher went checking on them in their neighborhood, it remained a mystery as to what had happened to the entire family. They had simply vanished, leaving pets and belongings behind. Soon after, I heard adults whispering between themselves:

"The Germans are picking up the Jews at home, at work, and on the street."

"Where are they taking them?" one would ask.

"Nobody knows," another would answer.

Then, shaking their heads in resignation to an unknown problem that they could not solve, they quickly changed the conversation to a topic more important to their own lives. I myself never pondered the fate of two schoolmates I hardly knew. Besides, daily survival exhausted me and my family enough, leaving us no time or energy to worry about others.

All those thoughts were swirling in my head when I realized I had arrived at the last house of the complex where I hoped my little sister had found refuge. The woman who lived there alone attracted young children to visit her by reading them stories. My friends and I spent entire evenings during the cold winter months, talking freely and endlessly about anything, all cuddled around her hot wood-burning stove, our cheeks red and warm. My sister, as I had suspected, was indeed there, sound asleep. The woman besieged me with questions as soon as I entered and let me go only when I promised to come back later with more details. This was a promise I never intended to keep.

Grand-mère had finished preparing dinner and was anxious to see us sit around the table, but it felt very strange, almost a sacrilege to start eating without our parents. We always took our meals together, and the two empty seats staring at us made us feel ill at ease. I understood Michel's determination to go away, but "how will we know what has become of our parents if we leave too quickly? How will they find us or where will they go if they are set free?" I asked myself.

I was struggling with all those problems when the door sprang open and astonishingly, my mother walked in, tired and drawn and out of breath. Here is what she told us as soon as she sat down.

She and my father had been driven to the town jail and thrown into an empty room with no windows. Soon after, two guards and a civilian came in and immediately started to question my father, who sat in a chair in the middle of the room, his hands in shackles behind his back. They wanted names—names of anyone he knew or suspected to be connected with the Resistance, names of anybody who took walks at night, names of suspicious neighbors, co-workers or young people meeting regularly after curfew. They wanted my father to denounce someone, anyone. Their shouting grew louder as my father kept quiet.

One guard threw a punch; another joined him and the two of them started to beat up my father with their fists and feet. My father fell on the floor, blood running down his face. My mother was screaming, imploring them to stop, but the guards, carried away by a savage frenzy, did not seem to hear or care. The civilian man was urging my mother to tell whatever she knew. She could only repeat that she was the guilty one; my father had done nothing wrong.

At long last, a German officer entered the room and snapped a few orders in German. My mother watched the guards drag my father's body out of the room. He seemed lifeless. Numb and in shock, my mother crawled on the floor, trying to follow them, but the guards pushed her out of the way and locked the door behind. Hours passed and she stayed, prostrate on the floor, waiting for the guards to come back and interrogate her also. Instead, the same German officer who interrupted the beating came in and helped her to her feet, telling her in perfect French to go home.

Bewildered, she asked to see my father before leaving but the officer refused. Still, he assured her that her husband had regained consciousness and was expected to recover from the wounds. He would be sent to a prison camp in the northeast of France, close to the German border. In the meantime, he ordered my mother to come back early the next morning and bring my father's ration card and other papers.

Too weak to get up the next morning, my mother sent me instead. The jail, a big, circular, high-standing gloomy building, stood on the opposite edge of town. It meant a few kilometers walk one way. I arrived before noon and felt chills when I walked the long driveway and confronted the stern dark walls and bare windows. My heart felt heavy at the thought that my father lay in one of those dreary rooms, feeling hardly alive, simply because my mother burned some pantry shelves and other furniture belonging to the landlord, so she could keep us warm on a cold winter night and cook our meager dinner.

I handed my papers to the man sitting at a desk at the entrance. He seemed kind, so I begged him to let me see my father. His answer was a firm "No!" and he told me to leave immediately. As I was slowly going around the prison walls to reach the main street, another tall man riding his bicycle caught up with me and started a strange conversation.

"How does it feel to have a father in jail? You should be ashamed of him. Who are his friends? Do you see them sometimes? What are their names?"

Names again! "Why do they want so many names?" I wanted to walk faster on the sidewalk, but he kept up with me by pedaling harder and continued with derogatory remarks about my father, whom he probably never had met. This despicable man was making me cry and I silently hated him. At the intersection, I ran across the road and walked against traffic. He could not follow me anymore. I saw him turn around and ride his bicycle back toward the jail, where he disappeared.

When I walked into my house later that afternoon, my mother was asleep. She slept on and off for days but finally snapped out of her torpor and slowly prepared herself to go about finding a job.

The German soldiers never came back to check on us, and Michel gave up the idea of moving us children to my grandparents' village. Our father was in our thoughts constantly, but we avoided talking about him as it brought more sadness and sapped our energy. Deep inside, we all feared we would never see him again but kept silent about it. Then, one day, a glimmer of hope came our way.

My father had a sister, his only sibling, ten years older than he. She lived up north on the coast, and when she heard her brother was detained close to the German border, she arranged a trip to the town nearest his prison camp. After many *pas et démarches,* or much red tape, she was granted a short visit which lasted only a few minutes, but what a wonderful vision she reported to us! Not only had my father seemingly recovered from his brutal beating, but he also looked healthy, energetic and in good spirits. We welcomed the news, and in spite of having no more contact with him (subsequent visits were denied and our letters went unanswered), we kept hoping his good health would persist and he would not be sent to another camp. We eventually stopped thinking so much about him, overwhelmed by our own daily chores and efforts to stay alive.

Chapter 9

Mother Works for the Enemy

Like most women of her time, our mother had never worked outside the home before. Growing up on the farm where she labored alongside her brothers, she never developed any special skill, and only had a few years of elementary education. Therefore, she inevitably approached the "Help wanted" ads of our local newspaper with great apprehension and frustration.

Initially having no success, she was on the brink of desperation when someone suggested she should try selling that very newspaper. A chosen location uptown was offered her. The last young man who held the job before had quit, as he feared a German patrol could spot him and deport him to a labor camp in Germany. No other man would replace him. My mother, eager to earn a paycheck, immediately accepted the challenge. Later on, to supplement her income, she also took a part-time job in a restaurant nearby. Proudly, she paid the rent on time the following month.

Unfortunately, her long working hours kept her away from us more and more; we were asleep when she came home at night and she was already gone when we woke up in the morning.

Weekends proved even more demanding when the restaurant stayed open late in the evening. We felt lonely every time we sat around the dinner table. The conversation grew tiring. I adjusted painfully at seeing an empty chair next to mine where my father used to sit, but when my mother stopped eating her meals with us altogether, it made another void. Grand-mère did not feel well, and I decided to use this excuse, one afternoon, to surprise my mother with a short visit. I had not seen her for days.

As I walked toward the square where she usually stood, I heard her voice rise high above all other noises of the street. "*La Dépêche! Les dernières nouvelles!*" (The latest news!) she shouted over and over again.

I stayed hidden at the corner of the building to take a peek. It had been raining earlier and my mother, standing on the sidewalk near the curb, looked wet. Her clothes clung to her body and her straight hair dripped. Then, in her rush to serve a customer riding his bike in the street, she stepped into a large puddle, soaking both feet. Seemingly unconcerned or ignoring her discomfort, she kept brandishing the newspaper high in the air and shouted its name: "*La Dépêche!*"

Saddened by what I saw, I hesitated to run to meet her. I knew she would disapprove of anyone disturbing her while she worked, especially when she did not look or feel her best. "Today is not the right day for chatting," I told myself. Nevertheless, after a few minutes of collecting my thoughts, I bounced back on the sidewalk and greeted her with a loud: "*Bonjour, Maman, c'est moi.*"

Startled, she turned around and quickly showed her displeasure by scolding me: "What are you doing here? Should you not be at school?"

I gently reminded her that on some days, I only had morning classes. We had to share our classrooms in the afternoon with other students whose own school had been requisitioned by the German army. The soldiers needed dormitories. As I kept talking, her face softened and I perceived a smile. She went on to explain it had been a bad morning for her. The rain had kept the people away and she still had a large bundle of papers to sell. There would be no time for her to rest before running to her second job.

Watching her more closely I noticed she had lost weight. Her eyes looked tired. I could even read the pain on her face when we started to walk. "My legs hurt," she admitted.

I had always known my mother could not stand or walk for an extended length of time without suffering intensely. (A back injury she incurred as a child, I was told.) I offered to stay and help but she refused vehemently, so I left, feeling very troubled.

On my way home, I caught up with Jeannine. She, too, had been wandering in town, doing some errands, on her half day off from school. We proceeded to walk together along the canal like old times, but sensing my absent-minded state she asked softly, "What's the matter? You are not very cheerful today. Aren't you happy to be away from school?"

"Everything is wrong," I answered with a sigh. "My mother works too hard, does not get enough sleep and I think she is sick. She needs a better job but can't find any," I blurted out in one breath.

Jeannine listened quietly while I unloaded all my worries to her. It felt good talking to her and by the time we arrived at our homes, I was laughing again.

A few days later, a man stood on our doorstep: Jeannine's father. He claimed to have great news for my mother so we let him in. While he sat down on the chair that Michel was offering him, he explained with excitement.

"Jeannine, my daughter, has told me about your predicament. At the moment, I am working at the German factory that you can see from your back yard and I know of a job opening perfectly suitable for your mother. It's a sitting down position and I have arranged an interview for her."

Not only did he wait for my mother to come home that night and tell her whom to see at the plant, but he also coached her as to what to say.

Full of confidence, my mother went the very next day and to her amazement, was hired immediately. She was going to be part of a team making ammunition for the German army!

A little dazed by the speed of things and perplexed at the outcome, I did not fully rejoice at my mother's good fortune with the rest of the family. I thought about my father. Twice he had quit his job, refusing to work for the Germans. What would he think if he knew?

But then, I saw my mother regain her health and her youthful spirit. Oh! How she loved to play games with us children, whenever we had a free moment together. "Hide and seek" remained one of her favorites. Our apartment consisted of only two rooms with not much furniture, but she always found the most unusual places to hide both my brother and sister and took pleasure at seeing me search for them. Once, I found Michel on top of the large armoire where she had nestled him between blankets and pillows while Lucienne was all cuddled up in the laundry basket. During those times, life had some sort of normalcy again. I struggled at the thought, but I came to understand that survival was to be our prime goal even if it meant working for the enemy.

Chapter 10

The African Prisoners

About a week after my mother started to work at the factory, Michel and I, along with all the other children of the neighborhood, became suddenly intrigued by a new group of black men, huge in stature, who played soccer in an enclosed field right behind that factory. We saw them every day around noon from the railroad tracks, our path to go back and forth to school. Their loud cries of excitement, so explosive at times, scared the bravest of us. We had never seen African men before except in pictures in our geography books or in a movie in the local theater, and we were glad to see that a large body of water at that spot separated us from this rowdy group. Michel was curious, though, and very eager to learn more about those strange but fascinating men. He developed the habit of waiting at the gate for our mother at the end of the day just to catch another glance of the group as they returned to their barracks.

One such evening, Michel persuaded me to go with him, and while we waited at the entrance of the factory, he engaged in a friendly conversation with the German guard familiar to him. It started to rain and the guard kindly opened the gate to let us take refuge under a shelter inside the compound. But no sooner had the guard returned to his post than Michel darted out across the camp in the opposite direction of my mother's building. "Come on, run!" He yelled at me.

On an impulse, I started to run also, trying to catch up with him, completely bewildered at what he was doing. German soldiers appeared at every block. I expected to hear shots aimed at both of us but nothing happened, so we kept running. Where is Michel going? I asked myself, nearly out of breath.

Abruptly, he stopped at a building next to a side door that was wide opened. He paused for a few seconds, then bravely went inside. Too frightened to follow him or to turn back and face the guard, I waited furtively at the entrance. I could hear men with deep voices talking inside. They spoke French, educated French, with no slang or profanity. I concentrated so hard to define their distinct accent, that I never heard the noise of another group approaching behind me until it was too late. "Oh, look! We have a girl here!" I heard someone exclaim.

Then all at once, a crowd engulfed and pushed me inside. When I found my balance again, I was in the mist of giant black men with broad smiles and sparkling white teeth, talking very loudly. Terrified, I felt faint. But then, the one nearest to me made my fear go away by showing some concern, "Are you all right? What's your name? You are new here, aren't you?"

"I am looking for my brother," I managed to articulate.

Gently, he led me away from the unruly men still blocking the door and invited me to walk through the room on my own.

"Go ahead," he insisted. "You are safe."

After my eyes adjusted to the dim light and my composure returned, I discovered a long room filled with beds neatly lined against the walls. Wood tables and benches ran in the center from one end to the other. Men sat there, either eating or writing. Someone passed near me holding a plate steaming with food. The strong aroma of exotic spices made me sneeze. Other men were quietly busy tidying things around their beds. They greeted me with a smile or a nod of their head as I walked by. No one seemed disturbed or surprised by my presence. A group emerged from somewhere in the back making a boisterous entrance. To my horror, I noticed they were half-naked, wrapped only in a large white towel. Each carried a small bundle of neatly folded clothes. I stepped aside to let them march by as they came toward me. So immersed were they in their jovial conversation, they did not even notice me.

What a strange place this is, I thought. Are the men used to visitors dropping in unexpectedly? And where is Michel?

My eyes searched the place up and down, but could not find him. I was ready to leave when I heard his voice coming from the far corner of the room. "Oh! I found Senegal and here is French Congo. But where is Guinea?" I heard him ask. A wave of laughter buried the rest of his voice.

What is Michel talking about? I wondered.

Squinting my eyes to focus more sharply on the men standing around him, I caught a glance of my brother crawling on his hands and knees. A large man hovering over him pointed to something on the ground. Curious and alarmed at the same time, I walked straight to the spot. I found my brother examining a map of Africa crudely drawn on the cement floor. Some men were directing him in finding the names of villages they left behind, while others patiently explained how, when France declared war against Germany back in September 1939, their own countries—then colonies of France—sent them to fight on the German border. Taken captive almost immediately, they found themselves in prisoner of war camps in Germany where the harsh weather killed many of them the very first winter. The others, too sick to work most of the time, were repatriated to various locations in France where the climate proved more tolerable.

Though they spoke the same language as the local people and were allied with the French, their sheer stature and flagrantly dark skin color made it impossible for them to escape. They would be recognized immediately wherever they went and be captured again. But then, for the same reason, they enjoyed a lot more freedom than regular prisoners of war. They were allowed to leave camp when off duty and roam around town as long as they came back before curfew. They could also receive visitors, and were delighted to see children.

"*A table, tout le monde!*" someone summoned, and the men jumped to the table where food had been served. Michel followed. A plate was set in front of him and he started to eat. I knew all along my brother had a knack for making friends and finding food, but this time I was amazed at the speed of his success.

"Michel," I called softly. He turned around, completely baffled to see me.

"What are you doing here, Odette?" he exclaimed. "Only men live in these barracks."

"I noticed," I retorted. "Why did you leave me at the door? And what are you eating?" The smell of food was making me hungry.

"Mutton, with rice in a red sauce too spicy for you. But here is a fruit bar I know you will like." He handed me a sticky piece of dehydrated fruit wrapped in a cloth, which he pulled out of his pocket.

The man next to him moved a little to make room for me on the bench and more dates and figs and other exotic sweets unknown to me came my way. A feast!

Finally, it was getting late and we prepared to leave. Crossing the room again, I noticed peculiar things I had missed the first time: sheepskins were spread on the floor at the bottom of each bed, and here and there, men were prostrating themselves on them. I realized they were praying, but because I never witnessed anyone demonstrating their faith in this fashion before or even anyone praying outside a church, I kept watching, mystified.

"Let's go," my brother yelled, breaking the spell.

As we reached the side door we had used to come in, I heard muffled sounds coming from behind the back wall a few feet away. When I got closer to explore, I came face to face with the barrel of a gun sticking out through a slit. In fact, the whole wall was dotted with slits, and eyes were watching me. As I looked up, I discovered a small door and window through which German guards had perfect view of the African prisoners. Germans lived there day and night, in a back room, right on the premises. Our African friends moved around under constant surveillance.

Michel and I visited their barracks many times after this first adventure. We always went back home with our pockets full of exotic sweets and dried fruits that we shared at mealtime for dessert. The two German guards encamped next door became less frightening than we first thought. We bravely pushed their door open once and entered their small kitchen. Happily surprised, they crouched next to us, put their arms on our shoulders and, softening their voices when talking to us in German, made us understand we were welcome. They closed their eyes when Michel grabbed a few slices of dark bread on his way out which he offered to me later, saying, "Here, this is for you. It's good bread."

Our African friends disapproved of us visiting the guards in the back of their barracks. They reminded us constantly that the Germans remained our enemies, no matter how kind some appeared to be. Then my mother worried endlessly about the increasing boldness of my brother, who was determined to come home some night with the whole loaf of bread. She feared that the German guards might lose their patience and chase him all the way to our doorstep. Under her insistence, Michel and I eventually stopped altogether entering the factory compound. Instead, my brother invited some of the youngest African prisoners to visit him at home, and have dinner with us, occasionally.

Chapter 11

Sister Marie-Thérèse

Several of my classmates were preparing to receive their first Holy Communion according to the Catholic faith, the predominant religion of France. They talked at length about relatives coming to witness the big event: a grandmother, an uncle, an aunt, some cousins and a few friends. All expected at least one gift. I envied them.

I knew we were Catholics. The small crucifix hanging on the wall in my parents' bedroom proved it. Also, the baptismal certificates contained in the box my mother carried with her during air raids showed that my siblings and I had been baptized in the faith soon after birth. Then, of course, I was aware of my mother's ritual. She always sketched the sign of the cross with her knife on the back of any new loaf of bread before cutting the first slice. Her way of thanking the sky for having food to eat that day, I thought. So, why wasn't I preparing for first Holy Communion along with my peers?

My mother's constant ritual was the only visible religious sign in our household. Like most people I knew we never went to church. Only my grandmother did, and whenever I visited her, she took me along to attend mass on Sunday mornings in the only church of her village, and always proudly introduced me to all her friends. With my head coifed with one of her black hats which inevitably fell halfway down my face, as they always were too big for me, I walked beside her, holding her hand tight so I would not trip over obstacles. I eventually persuaded my mother to buy a more fashionable, all-occasion scarf for me, which I used to cover my head when I entered the church, complying with the rule of the time.

I had not forgotten the African prisoners, and the image of them using sheepskins as prayer rugs haunted me. I harassed my mother with questions. "Why do they pray that way? What is their religion? Who is Allah?"

Completely bewildered by my sudden curiosity about religion and confronted with the fact that I had reached the age when most children in France took an important step in their religious life, my mother went to talk to the parish priest.

Father Bernard wasted no time. Arrangements were made immediately. A nun was sought to tutor me once or twice a week at no charge. With her help, Father Bernard assured us, I would be ready to receive my first Holy Communion in time with my contemporaries. So, on the very next afternoon, since I had only morning classes at school, I marched straight across town to meet Sister Marie-Thérèse in her convent behind St. Peter's church.

It took me forty minutes to reach the square where the church stood. Once there, I went around to the back, climbed the large steps that went up to a narrow street, crossed to the other side and found the twisty, tortuous little passageway my mother said would lead me to the convent.

The path took off rather steeply between two old buildings and the huge cobblestones under my feet, uneven and eroded, made walking treacherous. The walls, covered with centuries of grime, looked black. The jagged stones nearly choked the little road itself at the first turn where one of them protruded sharply halfway across, making the passage even narrower at that point. As I squeezed through, touching the dark walls with my fingertips, I felt the dampness. Moss grew in the crevices. At places, gravel fell and piled up at the bottom of the decaying wall. The sun shone in the sky, but the pavement stayed damp and dark, untouched by the warm rays, which reached only halfway down the side of the building. Out of breath, I tried to lean against the nearest wall for a minute's rest but felt an uncomfortable bump against my back. Checking it out, I noticed the wall bulged at the base, as if collapsing under its own weight. Across the way, windows cut high above and deep into the stone had bars on them instead of curtains, and like the street below, ran long and narrow.

Who lives behind those gloomy walls? I wondered. With no lamppost in sight, I shuddered at the thought of crossing this part of town at night in complete darkness. A remnant of a medieval past, the area felt ominous. Where is my mother sending me? I wondered.

Somewhere in this labyrinth of alleyways, a convent sequestered itself and I had to find the entrance. It did not take long. I came to an intersection where the road divided. As I stood there deciding which way to go, my eyes fell on a tall iron door at the corner straight across from me. Big letters just above it caught my attention and I walked to it. It read: *Couvent des Ursulines.*

This was the place! I had arrived at my destination. I pulled the cord that hung on the side and heard a bell echoing everywhere behind the wall. A buzzer released the door immediately and in I walked. A flight of stairs going straight up to a higher floor confronted me on my left. I started climbing again. Some fixture attached to the wall provided a dim light. Finally a large desk appeared at the top of the stairs, and a face rose above it slowly, as if trying to find me. The face looked so stern and so white in the gloomy light, that it frightened me. Certain I had just disturbed a ghost, I started to run down as fast as I could. I stopped when I heard someone call me back:

"Odette! Are you Odette? We are expecting you. Please, come on up."

I turned my head sideways and saw a nun standing at the edge of the landing. All wrapped in black, tall and thin, she looked eerie in the semi-darkness. "There is my ghost," I heard myself mutter.

Nevertheless, with her hands extended towards me, she seemed more inviting as she kept talking: "Sister Marie-Thérèse is having her lunch. Did you have yours?" she asked.

"No." I said. "I live too far away from school and did not have the time to go home."

"Then, follow me," she ordered.

When I reached the top of the stairs again I noticed the long and narrow window just below the ceiling; it had bars and no curtains. My guide led me to a small room in the back and along the way I saw more windows of the same kind. A thought exploded in my head: "The nuns are the people who live behind those gloomy walls I saw from the street! The convent probably occupies several blocks of this old part of town."

I had been sitting for only a few minutes when a young novice brought in a plate filled with steamed potatoes sprinkled with parsley. "Sister Marie-Thérèse wants you to have lunch," she said simply while putting the plate on the table.

I devoured them immediately and nearly emptied the pitcher of fresh water the novice had added to my meal. I was just about to recline on my chair when a vision of happiness burst into the room. "I am Sister Marie-Thérèse," the vision said, "and will be your teacher for the next few weeks."

I could not believe my eyes. Sister Marie-Thérèse was young, pretty and vivacious. She talked with a smile in her voice and seemed to glide over the floor. Her footsteps made no noise. "Let's go to my favorite spot," she suggested, while grabbing one of my hands. Swiftly, she took me out of the room. I followed her through a long dark corridor that went deeper inside the convent. I was sure we were descending to some sort of a dungeon like the ones I knew existed in every old castle. Intrigued, I kept walking. At the end of the hallway, Sister Marie-Thérèse pushed a door open and we were splashed with sunshine.

"Wow!" I exclaimed in complete astonishment. We had arrived at a small but bright courtyard bordered with blooming flowers and green shrubbery. A strong scent of lilac filled the air and I heard birds chirping. Sparkling white pebbles covered the ground and in the middle, a large statue of the Virgin Mary greeted visitors. Other resplendent statuettes spaced here and there through-out the garden, stood like vigilant souls. It just looked lovely. I took a few more steps and marveled at the windows. Surprisingly low to the ground and fully opened to let the fresh air come in, they were adorned with curtains!

What a contrast from the ones I saw in the street, I thought. How could a convent which looked so sinister from the outside, feel so alive once one was inside?

A worn-out bench around the corner seemed to wait for people. Sister Marie-Thérèse led us to it. A patch of blue sky hovered over our heads. As I sat there looking up, I wondered if the nuns ever saw the planes, heavy with bombs, that flew regularly over our town. I wondered if they even heard the bombs exploding at night, as the thick walls seemed to muffle every sound.

Sister Marie-Thérèse had been watching me with amusement for quite a while. She sensed the scenery had a profound effect on me. Putting her hand on my shoulder, she whispered, as if telling me a secret: "I love this garden, too. I come here every time I need to sort my thoughts out."

There was not much teaching that first time. We chatted mostly. I think Sister Marie-Thérèse heard all the information she wanted at that moment, like the age and number of my siblings, the subjects I like best at school or the kind of work my father did. She learned everything about me in a short time while I learned nothing about her.

Week after week I visited the convent until early summer. Each time, a plate of steamed potatoes sprinkled with chopped parsley and a pitcher of water greeted me promptly. No variation. I was very thankful for each bite and still sometimes joke about the idea that Sister Marie-Thérèse bribed me to religion with bowls of steamed potatoes sprinkled with chopped parsley.

I grew fond of Sister Marie-Thérèse, the dark hallways, the back room where we studied, and the quietness of the convent. It felt safe there. The war stayed outside. I learned to appreciate the calm, orderly pace and tranquillity of the surroundings. At times, the convent attracted me so much, like a comfortable refuge, that with a little encouragement, I would have gladly dedicated my future to becoming a nun.

"No!" exclaimed Marie-Thérèse vehemently, when I confided my desire to her.

"Wrong reason, wrong time," she explained.

Soon afterwards, Sister Marie-Thérèse gave me weekly magazines to read. All told the stories of children about my age who died for their faith in some form or another. I was baffled. I did not understand the meaning of the material and stopped reading it altogether as I found it very demoralizing. Like everyone else, I was underweight and did not look well, but still planned to live. What was Sister trying to accomplish? Discourage me? As the weeks went by, I noticed she was becoming more distant, but nevertheless kept her promise to continue my religious instruction and eventually I graduated in time to receive my first Holy Communion with my peers. On the eve of the big day we both went to the garden to sort our thoughts out. Sister Marie-Thérèse seemed reserved and I sensed then that I would never see her again.

Communion day came and passed. I remember being dressed all in white and feeling sad all day as I missed my father. No distant relative had been invited, not even my grandmother. There was no special celebration at home and I received no present. Still, when I went to sleep that night, I felt content and silently said "thank you" to Sister Marie-Thérèse for a good day.

When I returned to the convent for a visit at the end of the summer, Sister Marie-Thérèse was no longer a resident. No one would give me any explanation. A few years later, the convent closed.

Of course, I never became a nun. I married and had six children instead. But in my tumultuous life, many a time did I wish I had a convent to run to and a peaceful secret little garden, if only to sort my thoughts out. And yes, after searching and trying different Christian churches, I still find refuge in my favorite Catholic neighborhood church.

Chapter 12

My Visit to a Friend

My father had been on my mind a lot lately. I thought of him every day. I wondered if he was still alive and if we would ever see him again. We had no news. The tools in the shed reminded me of him constantly and it was painful to see the weeds take over his garden. We missed him, but did not dare mention his name at the dinner table for fear we would all break down and show our doubts about his survival. Still, I longed to talk to someone about him.

My mother had a girlfriend she had known for years. The two met quite often and sometimes my mother would bring me along to their afternoon outings whenever my school schedule allowed it. I liked Aunt Louise, as I affectionately called my mother's friend. A witty, mischievous brunette slightly on the plump size, but very well groomed and elegantly dressed, she was extremely attractive. Aunt Louise was also a gracious lady who welcomed me warmly each time I visited her. Unlike my mother, who frequently ran out of time and patience, Aunt Louise never seemed to grow tired of listening to my problems. Occasionally, she let me stay overnight or even spend a few days of vacation in her spacious apartment which I enjoyed immensely. It had electricity, indoor plumbing and hot water radiators which kept the rooms warm in winter. Aunt Louise and I could chat for hours on any subject I chose or about whatever troubled me. She was the friend I missed the most when we left town to go and live in the country, a good twelve miles away from her home. I remember borrowing my mother's bicycle several times then, just to go and see Aunt Louise and talk to her. I would embark on a deserted highway, brave the harsh weather of winter, and even pedal my way through unexpected enemy checkpoints with gusto. Moving back to the city more than a year later made my visits much easier.

So, when I woke up one morning with the strong desire to talk to someone about my father, I thought of Aunt Louise immediately. I was on my way to express to her how much I missed him.

I left my house in mid-morning. Taking the familiar path along the canal, I soon reached the street where Jeannine and I did most of our food shopping, then I cut across St. Peter's Square and went on and beyond the train station, where a dozen German soldiers stood and checked everyone's papers. I sneaked through easily.

An hour had passed by the time I finally arrived at Aunt Louise's apartment building on the far north side of town. After climbing the two flights of stairs, I was ready to knock on her door when I heard muffled cries coming from inside. Then shouting. I recognized Aunt Louise's voice: "How could you!" she kept saying. "Have you forgotten that your father is in a German prisoner of war camp?"

I heard a punch. Something or someone fell. As I stood there, puzzled and alarmed, I heard more sobbing. My hand rested on the doorknob. I turned it slowly and walked in. Then I stayed still, horrified by what I saw.

Monique, Aunt Louise's eighteen-year-old daughter, was curled up on the floor on her side and crying softly. She seemed to be protecting her stomach with her hands and arms stretched over it. Aunt Louise was in a state of rage like I had never seen before and kept on kicking her daughter with her bare feet anywhere she could. Her hands slapped here and there, too. Her face, all red with anger, looked distorted. And all along she kept on screaming, "Don't you know the Germans are the enemy? How dare you sleep with them! What are we going to tell your father?"

In a flash I understood. Monique was pregnant, and the father of the baby was the handsome German officer I met once when Monique and I took the dog for a walk one late evening many months ago, when I visited her. I still remembered vividly what had happened then.

We had crossed the deserted field that stretched along one side of the apartment building and continued our walk along a stone wall. It was dark and I felt very uneasy. I knew curfew time would soon force us to go back, but Monique and the dog kept going elsewhere. I silently wondered where.

Suddenly a soldier dashed out of the bushes and then, to my utter confusion, Monique's dog not only did not bark at the intruder, but ran toward him yapping happily. I stood still, bewildered, while the soldier and Monique embraced. I could not believe what I was seeing. I realized the soldier was German by the boots he was wearing, and his military hat told me he was an officer. I heard Monique explain to him who I was. I was terrified when he started walking toward me. He handed me a paper bag and said in perfect French: "*Pour le chien*." (For the dog).

When I finally dared raise my head to look at him, I found him tall and handsome and imposing, all at the same time. It was too dark to see his eyes, and I could only have an impression of his face. In no time Monique gave me the leash and the dog and told me to wait by the tree. Then the two lovers walked away. A few minutes later, I opened the paper bag and found bits and pieces of meat and a pastry. I gave the meat to my little canine friend, who begged soulfully. He was used to having a treat. I kept the pastry for myself. As I sat there all alone in the dark, I reflected on Monique's behavior and worried. I knew the French girls were attracted to the young, well-disciplined German soldiers whom they nicknamed "the golden boys," and threats of harsh reprisals floated among patriotic and furious French men. I was too young to date, but my mother had already warned me a hundred times that if I ever married a German, she would disown me. A lot of people felt the way she did.

After a while the two friends came back, just in time to get home before curfew. Monique and I and the dog left quickly while the soldier watched us safely cross the field again. On the way, Monique tried to justify herself.

"Hans is a kind man. He knows how hungry the French people are and he gives my mom loaves of bread to take home nearly every day. We share some of it with the family in the apartment underneath ours. They have such a hard time feeding their boys. Sure he is German, but he is not a Nazi. He hates the war as much as we do. His house back in Berlin has been bombed badly by the allied forces and he has lost several members of his family."

"How did you meet him?" I asked curiously.

"Mom works as a housekeeper in a nearby mansion requisitioned by German officers for their living quarters. They needed more help in the dining room at lunchtime so I applied for the job. Hans speaks French fluently and he seems to be the one in charge over there. I see him every day."

Surprisingly, by the time we arrived at the apartment that evening, I did not hate Hans as much. I was relieved to see Aunt Louise had retired to the bedroom already, otherwise she might have sensed how troubled I was and asked me questions. I had intended to stay a few days then, but I left the next morning.

Aunt Louise, who could not comprehend why I was leaving so abruptly that day, insisted in making me sandwiches to eat on the road. She also gave me a couple of dark loaves of bread to take home. I thought of Hans. Then she accompanied me downstairs to show me a back way through a myriad of gardens, so I would avoid German guards and checkpoints. Once outside though, I remember how frightened I became on that particular morning at the sound of gunshots and men shouting loudly. It sounded like a battle being fought just around the corner. Quietly Aunt Louise had pulled me to the side of the building to point out the field Monique and I had strolled through the night before. This time it was full of German soldiers practicing warfare. I remember watching their maneuvers for a while and noticing the big sign warning children not to play in the area.

"Those war games are a weekly routine," Aunt Louise had commented sadly. I had left quickly, full of mixed emotions.

On that day months ago, when I first met Hans, the German soldier, Monique had made me promise to tell no one. Not Aunt Louise, not even my parents. So I never did. I just stopped visiting as often, because I feared that I would spill the secret. I always wondered why Aunt Louise did not come to my First Holy Communion ceremony. Did my mother know? I had noticed the two friends did not socialize as much as they had in the past. But of course both worked full time nowadays.

And so there I was, now leaning against the wall in the dark hallway of Aunt Louise's apartment, having witnessed an ugly scene and recalling my previous visit, when a voice shook me out of my deep thinking. "Odette! Is that you? What are you doing here?"

I recognized Aunt Louise's boarder. He was coming home for lunch and he found me there in the dark corner of the entry way, still stunned by the fight between mother and daughter. In a daze, I followed him into the kitchen where Aunt Louise, seemingly calmed down by now, was setting the table, a stern expression on her face. She never smiled, which was so unusual for her. Monique had disappeared. Obviously neither of them had heard me come in, and they were completely unaware that I had watched part of their quarrel. I stayed for lunch, but of course, never mentioned my father, the real reason I came to visit. I felt a lot of tension during the whole meal and as soon as it was over, I went home. I did not feel like talking about my own problems any more.

Monique eventually had her baby—a beautiful healthy little girl, who in no time became the pride and joy of her grandmother, my friend Aunt Louise. Monique, the teenager who had foolishly fallen in love with an attractive young soldier from the wrong country, thankfully escaped the harsh, humiliating treatment endured by so many other girls after the war. Accused of having collaborated with the enemy, the girls were dragged nude in the street, their heads entirely shaved, and paraded for everyone to see by ex-maquisards who would not forgive. Because wigs were not always available, those unfortunate girls relied on scarves for months afterwards to hide their bald heads. No matter where they went, people could easily recognize them and shame them again. Monique fared better. She married a Frenchman before the birth of the baby, and the new family moved away, unscathed.

When I made a 1996 trip to my homeland, I located our family's wartime downtown apartment.

One of the neighborhood gardens where, tormented by hunger, I ate strawberries.

A poignant stop on my 1996 trip was the pastry shop where my risk-taking brother got angry at a German soldier.

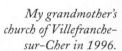

My grandmother's church of Villefranche-sur-Cher in 1996.

Chapter 13

Remembering Father

It was early afternoon when I left Aunt Louise's apartment, and because no one at home expected me to be back before dark, I decided to visit the downtown neighborhood where we lived when the Germans came, before we moved away to the country. "I can tell everyone about Monique being pregnant tonight at the dinner table," I told myself. "Now I don't have to keep that old promise."

At the train station I aimed for the high and windy passageway that helped the pedestrians cross over the multitude of railroad tracks. I saw a train in the distance coming in slowly. I wanted to stay and watch it pass underneath and then observe the passengers step in and out, but the sight of German guards walking back and forth along the tracks below, stopped me from lingering. I quickly stepped down at the end of the passageway and reached the busy avenue that goes straight to the center of town.

At the *Près-Fichaux,* as Bourges calls its beautiful gardens, I turned left and entered the park through the big gate. The landscape, the flower beds and green borders had been a joy to see before the war, when our whole family came for a stroll on Sunday afternoons and met friends. The playground brought back more memories. This is where I found my first colorful, small bouncing ball discarded by another child the night before. I sometimes ventured on my own early in the morning in search of forgotten toys. Back then, we lived only five minutes away from the park. In fact, as soon as I raised my head like I used to while standing on a certain spot just outside the gardens, I clearly saw our third floor apartment window again. Wide open, it showed another family lived there. I did not envy them. The apartment was dark and gloomy.

In a few minutes I reached the city market, crossed the street, and then turned into the little back alley going to the brewery. I recognized the strong smell a block away and when I glanced into the courtyard, I saw the usual horses and wagons the men used every day to transport their goods. I had heard some of the horses had been requisitioned by the French Army and forced to go to war too, along with the men. Had they survived their trauma and come back? At the end of the alleyway, I came across the tiny square where I spent so much time playing with the other children, and there to my left, was the doorway from which I had seen German soldiers for the first time. I entered the courtyard. It was empty. But my head filled up instantly with old images.

All at once, I visualized the crisp early morning a few years back, when the neighbors gathered around my father, there, at the spot in the yard where I was standing at the moment. They were touching him, looking at him, while talking with low voices. He was dressed in a soldier's uniform. I had never seen him dressed that way before and it startled me. He explained that he was going "to fight bad men."

"He is going to war," a lady added, nodding to me.

I did not understand either one of them, but the grave look on my parents' faces frightened me. Another man appeared also dressed as a soldier. I recognized him as a friend of the family.

"Time to go," he signaled to my father, and after more handshakes and "*Au-revoirs*" the two departed. The group of adults lingered a little longer in the yard, whispering and shaking their heads, and then quietly everyone went back inside their apartment.

I do not know how long my father was gone, that time, or how far north he went, but it seems that only a few days had passed when I heard people shout in the street:

"France has surrendered! The fight is over. Our soldiers are coming back."

Indeed, our soldiers were coming back, but how pitiful and beaten they looked! Disheveled, exhausted, they crossed our town, all alone or in small groups, hoping to arrive at their towns or villages before the enemy closed all the roads. Some sat on the curb to rest a while and accepted the food people gave them. Others took their army shoes off, exposing their bleeding feet. I could still see in my mind the woman who walked up and down the street, that day, with a pail of water and slowly splashed it over the soldiers' sore feet. These soldiers had been retreating day and night, taking shortcuts across fields and rivers, trying desperately to stay ahead of the relentless German army. I saw one soldier rip parts of his uniform off and use the pieces to wrap his swollen feet. Then he threw his boots away. None of these men were soldiers by career. Like my father, they were civilians from all walks of life, recruited at the last moment. They might have never shot a gun, but it did not matter.

"We had no ammunition," I heard a soldier exclaim. "They gave us guns and nothing else; the supplies did not reach us in time."

People were shaking their heads in disbelief, unable to comprehend what really happened. It all had to do, apparently, with the Maginot Line. This reinforced defense system established after World War I on the northeast frontier between France and Germany had failed to work as expected. The German army simply came around through the adjacent Belgian border and attacked the French from the back by surprise. Thousands of French soldiers were captured. Taking advantage of the confusion and panic that ensued, the powerful German army continued advancing deeper and deeper into French territory and easily defeated the disorganized remnants of French military forces.

Like the woman with the pail of water I, too, went up and down the street looking at every soldier, searching for my father. He was not there. I remember how much I had worried about him back then, fearing that he could not walk fast enough and would be taken prisoner. For two days soldiers kept crossing our town.

Then on the third day, early in the morning, a familiar voice made me jump out of bed. My father! It was my father's voice. I ran to the kitchen. Dressed in civilian clothes, my father looked his usual self again. I noticed his military uniform neatly folded on the table next to his gun. He was waiting for the recruiting office to open so he could return it all, as ordered. My mother sat across from him, sipping a cup of coffee and listening to his every word. Louis, the friend who left with him, did not return. My father presumed he had been taken prisoner.

I respected my father. He was a hard working man, unskilled and with very little education, but he never complained. Orphaned at birth when his mother died suddenly and his father abandoned him, he was raised by farmers who trained him to work on the farm. At home, he divided his time between the factory and his garden. In wintertime, when the weather was too bad to work outside, he repaired our shoes, putting new soles on them. Lucky enough not to be captured at the onset of the war, he had miraculously managed twice to escape the German soldiers later on. One of those times was at the farm where he worked for a while, after we moved to the country. He had stepped into the woods for a few minutes when he heard the German trucks coming in the driveway. He had stayed hidden while they surrounded his friends and took them away. The other time was at the distillery soon after we moved back to the city, when my brother had insisted going with him one morning and had made him arrive ten minutes late. They heard the unmistakable and horrible sound of the German motorcade just minutes before entering the grounds and both hid immediately. Again, my father saw some of his co-workers being taken away.

My father was a quiet, thoughtful man. I remember the lesson he taught me one afternoon, when he found me gorging myself with plump strawberries in somebody else's garden. I knew of a little path that cut across well-tended gardens, and kept a vigilant eye every day on the ripening fruit. I also knew there would not be a lot of food to eat at supper that evening, as usual, and the red strawberries proved irresistible. After a quick survey to assure myself I was alone, I easily jumped over the fence and proceeded to fill my stomach. After a while though, I sensed someone watching me. To my horror, when I turned my head, I recognized my father standing by the gate, quietly observing me.

What is he doing here at this hour? This is not his usual route. What happened? Those are the thoughts that came to my mind immediately.

Nevertheless, I was caught and, fearing a scolding, I tried to defend myself. "I was hungry," I said simply, once back on the path next to him.

My father stayed silent for a few seconds, then stated: "The man who cares for this garden probably has children to feed too, and I am sure they are all as hungry as you are. You just ate most of their next meal."

Nothing else was said. No scolding. No spanking. For the first time, I realized other people were hungry too, and I never went again in someone else's garden to eat their strawberries. I did not have to. The following year, my father had planted all kinds of berries in our own garden and called me each time he discovered some ready to be picked. It was his quiet way of telling me he had not forgotten.

I knew how he and my mother met. She was tending some cattle in a pasture one day, while he was laboring in a field close by. "He liked what he saw" as he bluntly confided in me, and after only three following encounters, he went straight to my mother's parents to ask them permission to marry their daughter. She was seventeen years old and he was twenty-one. I was born not even a year later, and many of my friends envied me for having such young parents.

The courtyard in my old neighborhood was bringing back all kinds of memories. Painful memories. And they were all about my father. I wondered where he was at the moment. Still at the same prison camp? What about his health? Would I ever see him again? I missed him, terribly. Feeling sad, I started to leave the old city neighborhood. I did not meet any of my old playmates or neighbors, that day. Like my father, they were gone.

Chapter 14

My Brother and the German Soldier

As I was slowly turning the corner of our old familiar city street, I stumbled into my brother, who also had come impulsively that afternoon trying to recapture memories of a better time. Like myself, Michel missed having our father around. I had noticed how rebellious and restless he had become lately. Grand-mère complained about him nearly every night.

"I can't control that boy anymore," she would tell my mother. "He does not listen. He is always gone somewhere for hours and does not finish his chores." My mother would shake her head, looking worried, but had no solution.

It felt good to be with Michel after my bad adventure at Aunt Louise's apartment. We were walking through our *Rue Mirebeau*, making believe for an instant there was no war. We stopped in front of the shop where we used to buy our bread when we lived in the neighborhood, and I was savoring with my eyes the pastries on display behind the window.

"Do you want an apple turnover?" my brother asked, remembering those were my favorite treats.

"Do you have money?" I asked him, putting some sarcasm in my voice.

"Yes," he replied to my surprise. "I worked at the brewery the other day. I lied about my age and they hired me for a few hours, cleaning the yard."

So, that's where Michel spends his time, I thought. He was looking for odd jobs.

We entered the shop and stood in line behind the two other customers already waiting. When our turn came, Michel asked the clerk for the pastries we had chosen. At that moment a German officer entered the shop and everybody immediately cleared the path, letting the German approach the counter right away.

The clerk pushed our order aside and swiftly turned her full attention to the new customer. This officer did not speak French. He pointed to what he wanted. One of his desires was the exact pastry Michel had chosen for himself, two minutes earlier, and placed on the counter by the clerk. I saw my brother's face grow angry when the clerk wrapped it up and eagerly handed it over to the officer. Michel had a quick temper and I thought he was going to explode in words he and I would regret. I managed to calm him down by saying: "Wait! They probably have fresher ones inside." They did not.

"Come back tomorrow morning," the clerk apologized.

"Those Germans take everything away from us," my discontented brother grumbled while settling for something else.

Because our mood had changed, we decided to go straight home. I had walked towards home, a long way off, for quite a while and felt a little tired, so when I heard my brother suggest: "Let's ride the tramway," I agreed heartily. We would still have a long way to walk after the last stop at the edge of town as our house stood much farther away, but at least sitting down for twenty minutes or so sounded good.

As our usual stop was approaching, I stood up and slowly walked closer to the exit door. Michel stayed behind, his eyes fixed on a German soldier who also happened to ride the tramway and sat in front of us. I tried to get my brother's attention by calling him softly:

"Michel, we are there."

The tramway stopped. Some passengers got out, others climbed in, and the driver was closing the door when my brother sprang to his feet and to my horror, called the German soldier a loud *sale boche* or dirty *boche*—a slang word we used with hostility for all German soldiers. Then, he forcefully spit on the soldier's shiny boots before taking off running. He nearly knocked me down in the process. I stayed speechless. So did the other passengers. I think they were frozen in fear, expecting the German soldier to take some revenge on them. My brother's boldness had endangered all of us. The driver was aghast.

But the soldier reacted differently. He halted the tramway, which was slowly moving again, jumped out, and spotting my brother in the distance, chased after him. I saw both of them run down the street toward the local commuter train station, and enter the path next to the railroad tracks, which was our shortcut home. Michel, way ahead at first, was slowing down while the soldier ran faster and faster and was getting closer. I thought my unfortunate brother was doomed, when suddenly I saw him throw himself into the swamps and disappear in a patch of tall young willow plants growing there. The twigs moved violently as he went thrashing through them, and I followed his trail up to the middle of the narrow field where abruptly every movement ceased. "Michel fell into a hole," I told myself.

The German soldier stood at the very edge of the swamp, probably unwilling to go any farther and soil his uniform in the muddy ground. He stretched himself trying to see above the soft willows, on the lookout for any movement. Nothing.

I had followed the men from a distance, hiding myself the best I could in case the German soldier would recognize me and grab me instead. To go home meant walking past him, so I stayed crouched in the ditch, yards away, just beyond the curve of the railroad tracks. I feared he would see me though, in the clearing, if he decided to come back the same way, so I slowly crawled backwards till I felt I was completely out of sight. Then carefully, I went around through the gardens on the other side of the railroad tracks and came back to hide behind a clump of tall trees, keeping the soldier in plain view. Still no sign of Michel. Had he managed to escape by crawling away like I just did? Or was he patiently waiting for the German soldier to leave? I could only guess at what was going on.

Night came and the determined German was still there, squatted comfortably on the rails and standing vigil. His tenacity was unbelievable. I myself was getting sore, cold and hungry. I thought about my mother, who probably was extremely worried about not seeing us at the dinner table. We had never been so late. We were told to come home before dark, always. It was dangerous to wander around town after curfew hour.

I do not know how long I stayed motionless in the darkness, waiting for the soldier to leave, but when I finally heard his footsteps on the gravel, I sighed with relief. Still, I feared it could be a trick to lure my brother out, so I waited even longer. After an eternity I talked myself into slowly leaving my hiding place. I walked on the grass as much as possible to muffle my own footsteps. Here and there I stopped and listened, afraid that someone might be following me. The sky, the trees, the canal and the railroad tracks, all looked pitch dark. The night enveloped me. I was angry with Michel for his foolish behavior that had forced me to be out alone at such a late hour, and I worried about him at the same time.

It took me a long time to get home. I was exhausted. Then I had to face my mother as soon as I entered the house. She was sitting by the stove, waiting anxiously. When I explained what happened, she became frantic. "Come," she said nervously while putting her shoes back on. "We have to go and look for him. He might be hurt."

"What?" I answered vehemently. "My feet can't move anymore. Besides, it's too dark to see anything and I am too scared to go back over there."

At that instant, the door opened and Michel walked in, muddy, dirty, but unharmed. "I fell asleep," he stated, seemingly unconcerned.

A broom stood in the corner. My mother grabbed it and whack! I heard the broom crack over my brother's body. Michel did not even flinch. He only looked surprised, even amused. My mother, her nerves calming down finally, sent everybody to bed with a threat, "We'll talk about it tomorrow."

But she never did. I thought she had swept away the incident. I was mistaken. All along she was developing a plan to keep my unruly brother away from German soldiers and his other risky ventures, so we all could live more peacefully. I just never imagined it would involve me too!

It had been a long exhausting day. I collapsed into my bed.

Chapter 15

Off To The Farm

The school year was coming to an end, just in time to celebrate our country's national holiday on the 14th of July, commonly known as Bastille Day. Except that, because of the German Occupation, there would be no celebration.

I had been looking forward to the long summer vacation. Big plans were in my head. War or no war, this year I was determined to learn to swim. Already, the bigger boys in the neighborhood had shown me how to dive into the river and cross it by stretching and stretching and reaching ahead with my finger tips while holding my breath under water. Then, at two thirds of the way, when there was no momentum to propel me forward anymore, I had to stand straight up and reach the other side by walking on the riverbed.

"Just a few steps and your eyes and nose will rise above water so you can breathe," I had been told.

Daring, but great fun. We went back the same way. Miraculously, no one drowned, ever, and in due time the whole gang learned to swim, the oldest teaching the youngest, including Lucienne, my little sister, who earlier had given us a scare. She had ventured onto logs tied together and floating on the edge of the canal, where the men cutting the trees had thrown them. She slipped and fell, sinking into the water right underneath the bundles of logs. She could not swim. Fortunately, the two older boys in her group knew how, and did not hesitate to dive into the murky water to fetch her out. Later, the same boys taught her how to tread water and stay afloat. The children of Grand Mazières took care of themselves. We all met regularly at the river bend when the weather was too hot to do anything else, and we spent hours bragging about our latest feat, always eager to show off to each other our new skills. We all became fairly good swimmers.

I had collected a few books I intended to read in my free time. *Les Miserables* by Victor Hugo, my favorite author, was among them. During the long days of summer, I found it easier to escape somewhere outside and read for a few hours. At home, I took the risk of getting caught and having a few extra chores added to my load. I almost had to hide myself when I wanted to read a book during daytime hours.

"It's not healthy to sit down and do nothing for too long," I was constantly reminded by my father. "You'll become lazy."

So, it was with dismay that I heard my mother announce to Michel and me, one evening at the dinner table, "I have decided to send you both away for the whole summer to work on a farm."

"What?" I questioned, not fully comprehending what she was talking about. "What do you mean?"

"What farm? Where?" Michel echoed.

"I do not know what farm or where, yet," my mother answered, very calmly. "We'll find out tomorrow at the open market. Farmers come there every year at this time to hire children about your age to help during the harvest season."

I realized she was not bluffing when she added, "I will try to find a farmer who will take both of you together so you will not be separated. You will be safe in the countryside. No air raids there. And you will have plenty of food to eat. I have considered all of this very carefully."

My brother and I looked at each other, dumbfounded. What brought that all up? What prompted our mother to make such a decision? What wrong did we do that she wished to send us away? Question after question popped into my mind and then, all of a sudden, I knew.

"The German soldier!" I exclaimed. "Remember, Michel, how distraught our mother was that night when we came home so late and how furious she became when we told her what happened? She stayed very quiet about it the following days and we thought she had forgotten the whole incident. But she did not. The other night, when Grand-mère complained about you again for not being home on time, I heard our mother tell her to be patient as she was working on a solution. She found the solution. Michel, it's the farm."

My brother stayed quiet for a long time. I think he felt guilty. "It was my fault," he finally said. "Why is she punishing you, too?"

"I don't know," I answered. "Do children get paid when they work on a farm? Maybe she needs the money. But what kind of work can we do? I don't think I am strong enough to work in the field all day. Remember how tired our father used to get?"

We did not sleep well that night. I heard Michel twist and turn in his bed. I myself kept wondering what was going to happen to the both of us. I knew my mother was right claiming the farmers had more food to eat than we did. I witnessed it every week on my clandestine shopping trips to the near countryside. Of course, she was right about the air raids, too. No factories or airports or big train stations to attract the planes and their bombs every day as it did around the cities. Then, like my father, she grew up on the farm and was familiar with the custom of farmers hiring children at harvest time. All night long I tried to convince myself that spending the whole summer working on a farm was an exciting idea, but in the morning as I was trailing behind my mother and brother on the canal towpath, I kept hoping no farmer would want me.

I was wrong. As soon as we walked into the open market where farmers sold their products, a tall, slightly bent-over middle age man approached my mother as though he already knew what she had in mind. Apparently he liked what he saw, and before long I heard them exchange addresses and other information. A handshake sealed the deal, and in a matter of minutes we were sold for the summer to a perfect stranger.

Bright and early the next morning my mother, brother and I, with our little bundle of clothes, boarded the local train that would take us to the village where the farmer lived. He had hoped to give Michel and me a ride in his horse and buggy that very day when he met us, but my mother had insisted on taking us herself by train in the morning so she could see the farm too. Everything went so fast, I never had the chance to tell my neighborhood friends I would not be swimming with them this summer.

The train took us into a part of the country I had never seen before. The farmer was there, waiting for us as we arrived at our destination, and we all climbed into his buggy. The farm stood far away and it took a long time to get to it. I felt completely lost.

"It will be impossible for me to run away," I mumbled to myself.

We arrived at our new temporary home in time for lunch. We all sat around a long table and got acquainted with the farmer's wife who kept putting food on our plates. Another man, a regular helper, joined us and sat next to Michel. From him we learned that our new employers had no children of their own and every summer took in siblings to help with the work.

"You will like it here," he said, winking at us.

Our mother left soon after the meal, and my brother and I immediately went to tackle our new tasks. First, I helped with the dishes and swept the crumbs off the floor. Then, the farmer's wife and I led the sheep to a far-away pasture where we stayed for a few hours guarding them. The pasture was an open field in the middle of others, and every time the sheep strayed away across the borderline, we relied on our diligently trained dog to bring them back. In one afternoon, I learned to shout out all the right commands. I also learned to round my flock up at the end of its grazing time and guide it back to the farm, through dirt paths and the main road which, luckily, was always deserted. My sheep knew the way. I just followed them.

Michel had a dozen cows or so in his charge. He, too, took them to the pasture twice a day and watched them for hours all by himself. As we were always positioned at opposite corners of the whole farm, we never saw each other. Morning and evening he helped clean the barn, feed the horses and fill up the water bin where all the animals were led to drink at the end of the day. We were so busy we had no time to chat. Mealtimes brought us back together, but Michel sat with the men while I stayed at the other end of the table, and both of us could only listen to the adults' conversation.

That first night, we collapsed in our beds long before darkness. Michel and I had separate bedrooms, across the hall from each other. We thought of it as a luxury. Back home we shared the same alcove in the big kitchen. It was convenient in a way, as the kitchen was the only warm place in wintertime. I was still sound asleep the next morning, when I heard loud banging on my door and my brother's as well.

"*Debout!*" the farmer was yelling. "Time to wake up. It's 4:30 AM and we have to milk the cows." I could hardly believe it. I needed more sleep. I was still tired from the day before. Rubbing my eyes, I slowly joined the farmer's wife who was already preparing breakfast in the kitchen. I set the table. I sliced a loaf of hard bread in a soup tureen and boiling milk was poured over it later, with a dash of salt. A big platter of pork and vegetables found its way to the table next to a basket of bread and cheese and fresh fruits. There was more food displayed on that breakfast table than I had seen at home for lunch and dinner combined. In a flash, I thought about my father who got up at dawn every day and dreamed of a big breakfast. I finally understood why he liked so much to spend occasional weekends on the farm.

The days came and went uneventfully. The schedule stayed the same no matter what day of the week the calendar showed. Sunday was just another working day. The animals had to be fed and their stalls cleaned as usual. We were up before sunrise, took a short nap after lunch, and were asleep by 9:00 PM.

I cringed one late afternoon when I saw a man darting out of the woods only a few yards from where I was sitting watching my sheep scattered in the field. He walked straight to the farm and reappeared soon after carrying a large heavy bag. "Food!" I immediately told myself.

I was sure the man was a Maquisard, who came to collect some food for himself and his companions hiding in the woods nearby. I worried as I remembered my near encounter with the Gestapo in another farm some months before, and I hoped we would not be subjected to the same fate as those owners had. So it was with great relief I heard the farmer instruct his wife that night at the dinner table, "Don't give any food to anyone you do not recognize," he said with sadness. "It is too dangerous. Remember what happened to the Blanchards? They are gone. We don't see them anymore and their farm is empty."

The highlight of that summer on the farm, for Michel especially, came on the day the farmer and his friend, the village butcher, slaughtered a pig on a big table in the courtyard. It actually brought some excitement. Everybody helped, all day long. We cleaned, we trimmed, we brought pails of water and carried bags of crude salt, and then we watched the farmer's wife meticulously place all those pieces of meat in deep earthen containers with lots of salt in between.

"Meat for winter," the farmer acknowledged, with pride.

Summer came to an end and I was glad to see my mother when she arrived to take us back one morning. My heart jumped when I heard her voice coming from the yard as soon as the farmer let her out of his buggy. I had missed our little home and our own meager dinners, where we could talk freely about anything. I also had missed my friends tremendously. Every time I was alone in the field watching my sheep and feeling miserable in the hot sun, I visualized them splashing in the cool water of the river and having fun.

At my return, everybody marveled at my rosy cheeks. For the first time, I was the appearance of good health. What did I do the next morning? I slept!

Chapter 16

Grandfather's Vineyard

When our mother came to the farm to take Michel and me back home a few days earlier than expected, she had explained that our grandfather, or Grand-père as we called him, was running behind in harvesting his own grapes and needed our help. It was late September 1943.

"School will start soon, anyway," my mother pointed out. The farmer agreed and did not insist in keeping us any longer. He shook our hands to say "good-bye," and invited us to come back next year.

We rested two days at home sleeping late in the morning and off we went on the train again, this time to visit our grandparents. Our joy! Villefranche-sur-Cher, the village where our grandparents lived, stood a mere sixty kilometers away from our town, but the trip took nearly three hours. The train made all the local stops and was delayed midway by an air raid. Still, the familiar surroundings comforted us, and we took everything in stride. Villefranche-sur-Cher is located on the south edge of the Loire valley, that magnificent piece of land where the kings and queens of yesteryear built their summerhouses we call castles. Rich forests still attract avid hunters, and luscious gardens flourish everywhere. My grandfather had a small vineyard and made his own wine, and every year like a tradition, all his grandchildren big enough to work came to help him harvest his grapes. "Hard work but great fun," we told each other.

Our grandmother waited at the train station for us, and we all walked slowly to her house ten minutes away. There, two of my favorite cousins had already arrived. Seeing them again gave me a boost of energy. We talked late into the night even after Grand-père went to bed, Michel and I bragging about our hard work on the farm.

"Time to go to sleep," our grandmother finally ordered. "Tomorrow will be a long working day."

We woke up the next morning at the sound of our grandfather's talking outside to his two lasting work companions: a mule and a donkey. In his younger years, Grand-père had been a farmer with cows and horses in his barn. By the time I knew him, however, every animal and half the farm had been sold. As the years went along, the village had stretched, engulfing the surrounding land. Even the dirt road, which long ago ran by Grand-père's humble farm, had transformed itself into a lively main street with sidewalks and shops. Only the vineyard away up the hill and a few scattered vegetable gardens remained to keep Grandfather busy in his old age. A shelf in the storage room, stocked with jars filled with peaches, cherries and apricots, showed me the fruit trees were still producing and our grandmother had not lost her touch in canning.

We rushed through breakfast and hopped into Grand-père's sturdy wooden wagon. We cuddled close together on the benches on each side to keep warm in the early brisk, fresh air. That morning, it was the mule's turn to pull us gently to the field. At one point she stopped for some unknown reason and stubbornly refused to go any farther no matter how much Grand-père coerced her to do so from his seat. A few people gathered to watch. It was embarrassing. Finally Grand-père eased his long body out of the wagon and went to whisper a few words into the mule's ears while gently patting her on the head. It worked! The mule moved and the people applauded.

Grand-père was well known in the village and had many friends. Some of them greeted us along the way: "*Bonjour*, Eugene. How are you? Oh, I see you have helpers today."

"*Salut*," my grandfather would answer, raising his large hand at the same time.

Then the friends would invariably comment on how much we, the grandchildren, had grown during the past year and how fine we looked, which brought big smiles to our faces and a burst of pride in Grandfather's eyes. I liked Villefranche-sur-Cher. The village was full of old people who made young children feel good.

We soon reached the vineyard. Grand-père gave us each a basket and down the rows we went, bending, picking, singing songs and joking. After a while we quieted down, moving silently, totally immersed in our work. But then, one of us would break the spell by throwing a grape or two at a cousin trailing behind, and a short battle of flying purple bullets would ensue. Grand-père was always watching, though, and his cough, real or not, always made us stop. The grapes were terribly tempting and we ate our share. After a few hours, our tongues and lips looked purple, which made us giggle some more. Vine after vine, row after row, the baskets filled up. We brought them up to Grand-père, who waited for us at the top of the hill. He emptied the contents into a big barrel, and immediately crushed the grapes by whirling them round and round with a heavy wooden stick wrapped in a cloth at one end.

For five full days, we picked and carried baskets of gorgeous grapes until our backs ached, even after a good night's sleep. The mule and donkey took turns every day taking us back and forth to the field. One animal stayed in the barn resting all day while the other came to work with us. Like our grandfather, they were advanced in age and like him, they walked at a slow pace.

We went home for lunch to eat a copious meal cooked by our grandmother, usually consisting of a big pot of chicken or rabbit stew, a large green salad, a loaf of country bread and some goat cheese, and plenty of fruits for dessert. We talked happily and lingered around the table while Grand-père took a short nap. Then we all went back to the field for a few more hours.

Before leaving the vineyard each night, Grand-père would take a little walk through the rows, inspecting our work and evaluating how much was left to do. We knew he was satisfied when he winked at us on the way back. Grand-père never talked much. Still, it felt so good to be with him. Every day he made us fill a small basket of grapes to bring home for dessert or to give to the neighbors, while he himself went searching down the vines for the biggest and most luscious bundle of grapes he could find. Breaking it gently off the branch with his rugged hands, he carried it back to the wagon, placed it in a special basket next to him on the front seat and then offered it with pride to our grandmother. Grandmother never went to the field. She limped and walked with great difficulty. Grandfather simply brought the bounty of the field to her.

At the end of the third day, a new young wine begged to be tasted. Grand-père would line us up around him and give us a small glass of a bubbling clear refreshing liquid which we compared to grape juice. We liked it. It tasted sweet. No smell of alcohol at all, but two or three tries of it sent us giggling.

"Time to go home," Grand-père would say. "Another good wine this year."

It was hard to say good-bye to Villefranche-sur-Cher. The old people welcomed and cherished not only their own grandchildren but everyone else's too. Obviously they missed the village's young men. Most of them had left to join the resistance movement and fight the Germans, while others had simply been lured away by better paying jobs in a distant city. Still, no family felt lonely. Friends and neighbors kept in touch with one another. My grandmother never locked her door and regularly welcomed visitors stopping in for a few minutes' chat. She also caught up with all the village news every morning by simply walking to the bakery across the street or the little grocery store around the corner. Then, when the days grew warmer, she would pull a couple of chairs out to the sidewalk in front of her house, and wait for the more active elders who took a stroll after dinner. To her delight, a young family sometimes would stop by and all would share their concerns of the day.

I am very fond of Villefranche-sur-Cher. There, I learned to love and respect the elderly who were so kind to me, and to appreciate their slower, more serene way of life. No one I know now lives in the village. My cousins have long since moved away and my nearest relative, an old aunt, who gave me reason to return once in a while, is no longer with us. I can only visit her and my grandparents in the small cemetery where I am always astonished to read the names of so many young fighters all members of the Resistance—who died during the weeks following D-Day, liberating their own village and the surrounding ones from German soldiers. But that is ahead of our story.

After all those years, it feels good to reminisce about Villefranche-sur-Cher, my Grandfather and his vineyard, and the good times I had with my cousins despite the war, but can you keep a secret? Contrary to what my grandfather believed, no one in the family was very keen on his wine. For years, I heard the adults complain about it, between themselves:

"Too acid," my uncle, the connoisseur would say.

"It tastes like vinegar," my aunt would add with slight disgust.

Some even joked tenderly about Grandfather: "Our winemaker is getting too old; he has lost his taste buds."

But whatever they thought, they never told it openly, and went along with Grandfather each time he opened a bottle, took a sip, snapped the tongue a couple of times and said: " Ha! Good wine. Let's have a toast."

And all responded: *"A ta bonne santé, Grand-père!"* (To your good health, Grandfather!)

Chapter 17

A Knock on the Door

The night stood in deep silence; my whole family had been sleeping for hours. Winter raged outside in this early January 1944. My mother had filled our wood-burning stove with enough charcoal to keep us warm till morning. I slept, my head buried under the pile of blankets spread over my bed and my feet resting on the warm brick which had heated all afternoon in the oven. Wrapped in a thick towel, the brick worked better and longer than a hot water bottle.

Soft and muffled knocks on the door came to my ears as through a deep fog. They started to annoy me by their persistence. I tried to ignore them. But a stronger knock, louder and more imperative this time and followed by a voice calling from outside, woke me up completely:

"*Raymonde, c'est moi, Felix.*" From her back bedroom, my mother heard the knock and the voice. She flew out, ran past my bed in the alcove and glided over the kitchen floor. I had never seen my mother move so fast and so gracefully at the same time. Her bare feet hardly touched the floor, and her flimsy nightgown floated behind her making the whole scene a bit eerie in the dim light. All along she kept repeating:

"It's your father! It's your father!"

She reached the door in no time but, in her nervousness, struggled with the key. Finally she unlocked it and when she pulled it wide open, a silhouette emerged from the dark. The night intruder took one more step into the light and my heart recognized him instantly: "Father!"

I sat up straight in my bed, not believing my eyes. Stunned and speechless, I kept looking at him. My mother, too, had become numb with emotion. With her eyes riveted on the unexpected visitor, she stayed motionless in the open doorway, oblivious to the gusts of cold wind slashing at her. Time stood still for a few seconds, then my father walked in. A chair was in the way. My father grabbed it and slumped into it. He was tired. Someone closed the door. I heard my mother mutter a few words while she hovered all over my father, checking him out: "Felix, is this really you?" she kept asking.

Squirming next to me and rubbing the sleep out of her eyes, my little sister, Lucienne, pointed her finger and screamed in surprise: "Papa!"

She then jumped out of bed and ran to him immediately. I followed her. Michel was already there, wrapping a blanket around our father, who was shivering in his thin clothes. The whole family was up and gathered around the newcomer, looking at him in disbelief and touching him, as though we all wanted to reassure ourselves he was real. I think each one of us had slowly hardened himself to never seeing our father again. We let the thought escape a few minutes later, once we were able to mumble a few words, to which my father answered softly.

"Remember, I was sent to a prison camp on French soil, not a labor camp in Germany where so many die from sickness or overwork."

Because we did not completely understand the difference, he continued to explain, "The guards treated us fairly well. I enjoyed a great deal of freedom. I was allowed to garden so I grew a lot of vegetables. The other prisoners helped me, and all together we even had permission to set traps in the forest nearby and catch small game animals to enrich our diet. We all worked long hours every day, mostly outdoors in the fresh air," my father continued slowly, "but we managed to get enough sleep and plenty of food."

My mother, in fact, marveled at how healthy he looked and even thought he had gained weight. "You look so good," she said. "We worried about you constantly. We tried to imagine your life in the camp. We had no way of knowing how you were doing and sometimes we could not help but fear the worst. What if you became sick? Did they have a doctor in that camp?"

Then all at once, we bombarded him with even more questions: "What work did you do? When were you released? How did you get back here in the middle of the night? What if a German patrol would have caught you?"

"Did you escape?" my brother Michel inquired with, I think, excitement in his voice.

"No, no!" my father finally interrupted. "I was truly set free. Guards came to pick me up early this morning just as I was starting my chores. They took me to the main office. I thought I was being transferred to another camp, and it worried me. But to my surprise, an officer handed me my ration card, my civilian clothes, and a special pass and told me I could leave the premises. I did not move at first, because I thought it was a mistake or a terrible joke. Then he pulled out a train ticket and told me a guard was ready to take me to the train station. I had to hurry. They rushed me out while I was still in a daze and I am just as astounded as you are to find myself at home again. For one instant, I thought the war was over."

What we did not know then but learned many years later after the war, is that a powerful man had been watching over my father all along. A German retired officer had been in charge of our town jail at the time my parents had been arrested. This military man apparently had a conscience or a strong feeling for French citizens wrongly accused of anything and badly mistreated. Unable to stand against the Gestapo or other superior orders, he tried nevertheless to soften the blows by interfering whenever possible.

In the case of my father, he stopped the beating in time, had the wounds treated, and then sent my father to a camp he knew would be tolerable. Later, he reduced the sentence which had been for an "indefinite time" (meaning forever), and arranged my father's release. We came to suspect he was the officer who helped my mother to her feet after she collapsed from watching my father being battered on that dreadful day when both of them were arrested, the same officer who told her kindly to go home. The rumor persists that he helped other prisoners in the same fashion. He also gave a few more the freedom to communicate between themselves, while detained, and send messages to their families.

Of course at that moment we knew none of that, and for a long time we pondered the good fortune that prompted my father's return.

My father paused for a moment. Then, reflecting on his last day at camp he added, "It all went so fast and so unexpectedly, I never had the chance to go back to my bunk and say good-by to a few friends who, by now, must be wondering what happened to me. I wish I could remember their addresses so I could contact their families, but I left all my scrap notes behind."

In the meantime, my mother had rekindled the embers in our stove, made some hot chocolate and was filling the mugs that Grand-mère had set on the table. Then we listened some more to what my father had to say. "I am sure grateful for the train ticket, even if it took me only part of the way. The train stopped at Orleans. Everybody had to get out. I did not want to wait another day for a possible connection to somewhere closer, so I walked the rest of the way except when I managed to get a ride here and there, from farmers doing errands. Their horse and buggy carriages felt very comfortable. We traveled on dirt roads from village to village and never met any German patrols."

My father, warmed up and rested, continued talking for a long time. We were puzzled when he described to us one of his main chores. By an irony of sorts, this man who had been jailed falsely for chopping up the landlord's furniture to heat our kitchen and cook our dinner, was suddenly responsible for keeping the fires burning in every barracks and officers' quarters! He made his regular rounds, adding more wood or charcoal to every wood-burning stove. The German soldiers appreciated his work but at those moments he thought about us, and the reason he was there. He wondered how we were coping with the cold. He knew my mother had been released from jail. His sister, by surprising him with her short visit, had told him all the news, and it lifted his spirits to know that his children were not left completely alone. He never received any of our letters and never had the material or permission to write to us.

In good weather, he explained further, he cut logs in the forest and stacked them close by for further use and, in between, did a lot of yard work. His rugged, callused hands showed the wear and tear of his labor.

Then it was our turn to amaze my father by telling him how we had survived all those months without him, how my mother found a job at the factory, how quickly Michel and I had to grow up and become even more responsible, but also how much we had missed him, every day.

It felt good to hear my father's voice again. It felt good to have my whole family sit around the wood-burning stove for a few moments of peace. This time we had wood and charcoal to burn. No, the war was not over as my father had first hoped, but I fell asleep in my chair, dreaming that it was.

Chapter 18

My Uncle Raymond

I liked my Uncle Raymond. He was young, handsome and funny. He also owned a pastry shop, far in the mountains in the center of France, where I went on vacations once with my grandmother.

A week after my father's return from the prison camp, my Uncle Raymond paid us a surprise visit. It was lunch-time on a weekday, and we were all gathered around the kitchen table. We heard a knock on the door again, soft and puzzling. One we did not recognize.

"*Entrez*," my father shouted. The door was not locked, and my uncle walked in, a smile on his face. We jumped to greet him. His visits were so rare and impromptu that we appreciated each one of them.

My Uncle Raymond was my mother's favorite brother, the youngest in a family of six children. Like most of his older siblings, he left home at the age of thirteen to become an apprentice patissier (pastry man) with a family who stopped at his village one summer day, looking for a teenage boy willing to learn a trade. He went away to Paris with them where in exchange for room and board he worked as a helper in their shop. Years passed. By the time my grandmother went to visit him, she could hardly recognize him—he had grown so much. Occasional letters helped them to keep in touch.

After a long apprenticeship, my uncle became a good patissier himself. Living frugally, he managed to save enough money to buy his own patisserie, and moved to the mountainous town of Clermont-Ferrand, where the girl he planned to marry grew up. Not forgetting his parents, he traveled back and forth to his village at every opportunity, where I had the chance to meet him many times. I truly liked him. My father did too. The two of them could talk for hours, laughing and joking while munching on bread and cheese and drinking wine. That particular afternoon, they took a walk into town, and then to the train station where my uncle boarded a train to go straight back home.

This was the last time I saw him. Three days later, we heard that he was dead. The Gestapo came to his shop at dawn, a couple of mornings after he visited us, and seized him. My uncle had been working by his hot oven, baking large trays of breads and pastries for his daily customers. The soldiers barged into his shop, grabbed him and took him to jail without giving him the time to dress warmly. Being thrown into an unheated cell with no blanket or coat to protect himself against the frigid weather of winter, my uncle froze to death overnight. He was twenty-nine years old and died before the Gestapo had the chance to torture him.

Of course, we did not know all of that right away. The telegram only announced the death of my uncle and the date of his funeral. He looked healthy when we saw him last. Healthy and mysterious. People did not travel freely. They needed good reasons. To go on a short vacation or visit a far away relative very seldom earned you a pass. My uncle seemed to take many business trips but never elaborated on where he had been or why. He would just show up unannounced at someone's door, and rejoice at the happy surprise he created. Everyone in the family loved him.

To know more about his sudden death meant to go to his funeral. We had no time to waste. My parents decided to take me along with them, as I was so fond of my uncle. First, we would pick up my grandmother who was getting too old to travel alone. We all packed our own little suitcases and took off to catch the first train to my grandmother's village. Michel and Lucienne were left behind under the care of our resident Grand-mère.

As we had feared, our train was delayed because of sabotage somewhere on the tracks. It happened more and more in early 1944. We waited nearly two hours seated on a bench inside the train station before our scheduled train finally arrived and the guards allowed us to board. We were glad the rest of the trip was not canceled altogether.

"This is the local train; it stops at every village," my mother said. "It will take us another two hours before we reached Villefranche-sur-Cher to pick up your grandmother. Hopefully, we'll be there before dark and we can all catch some sleep before going to Clermont-Ferrand, first thing in the morning."

We never made it. Just a few miles before our grandmother's village, the train stopped. German soldiers came aboard and forced everyone out. They made us cross over deserted tracks and march in a long line toward several large buildings we could see in the distance. "Warehouses," my father said.

It was already getting dark. As we approached the buildings, armed soldiers immediately separated us: men were ordered to the right, while women and children were directed to go left. We had no other choice but to obey. I tucked right along, hanging on to my mother, while my father disappeared with the men. Some young children started to cry. "*Schnell! Schnell!*" the guards kept yelling at us. We were used to that favorite German command as it was thrown at us so many times. It meant "quick" or "fast" or even "faster," so we hurried.

Our group was pushed into a big warehouse where blaring lights hanging from the ceiling blinded us as soon as we entered. Huddled along one side of the building, we stood quietly, not knowing what to expect next. "Are they going to shoot us?" I asked my mother. She did not answer. German officers appeared in the room. "*Papeers!*" they shouted, then proceeded to check us out, one by one, looking at our faces, then at our papers.

When my mother's turn came, she eagerly showed her pass. We were cleared. But instead of being allowed to go back to the train, we were told to stay in the warehouse with the others until further notice. Then a guard came with a pile of pads and thin blankets and slowly distributed them around. We realized with anger that we were all going to spend the night in this huge warehouse. Why? No one knew.

Did the Germans need our train? Or had the tracks been sabotaged way ahead? Were the authorities looking for someone special? Those are the questions I heard people muttering about among themselves.

Resigned, we slowly settled down though, and tried to get as comfortable as possible, resting on a cold hard cement floor, drenched by glaring lights and surrounded by soldiers ready to shoot any one of us. Somehow, I fell asleep, to be shaken by my mother a few hours later: "Wake up! Wake up! We have to go," she was saying. When I looked up, I saw the guards walk up and down the rows, ousting the people and making them pick up their pads and blankets.

"Hurry!" my mother insisted, watching the guards kicking some of the slower passengers. The guards hustled us outside as swiftly as they shoved us inside the night before, with no explanation. But this time, they left us alone in the field to find our way to the train. Daylight was breaking. The men had been released a little earlier from their own warehouse and we found my father waiting for us just outside. He looked tired, drained. He said he hardly slept as he worried about us and about himself too. All night long, the guards took young men out, and my father never saw those men come back.

We walked to the train and boarded it. Twenty minutes later, we arrived at a relay station where another German patrol climbed aboard to check our papers. The train was delayed again. This time, it proved too much for my parents. We had already missed the funeral by one day, and traveling proved too unsafe. Therefore my mother decided she, alone with my grandmother, would attempt to finish the trip.

"You should not miss so many school days anyway," she added, looking at me. We separated quickly, and I followed my father in search of the next train returning home.

It took my mother one full week to get to Clermont-Ferrand. She and my Grandmother were exhausted by the time they finally arrived at their final destination. Daytime air raids on the trains by the Allied Forces, sabotage on the tracks by the Resistance, and endless German patrols caused all the delays.

A month later, my mother was back with us. She confirmed what we had suspected all along: My Uncle Raymond was part of the Underground movement. Made up mostly of patriotic French young people, the Underground was responsible for derailing countless trains or slowing them down in order to stop the transportation of French goods to Germany. Those young men and women moved from place to place incognito, with false papers, and slept overnight in different homes considered safe.

I remembered my uncle's stairwell. It went up to the third floor. During a short vacation at his house, I saw my uncle one late night carry a plate of food up to what I thought was the attic. I even heard muffled men voices. Intrigued, I tried to explore this upper floor the next afternoon and started to climb the stairs. My uncle caught me, called me back right away and scolded me harshly.

"You must never go up there. It's forbidden. Next time, I will spank you."

So, I never did. But later, much later, I told my parents. And they guessed immediately that my uncle's house was used as a safe haven for Maquisards. We presumed some of them were eventually caught by the Gestapo and tortured until forced to give names and addresses, including Uncle Raymond's location.

We learned all of this after the war, from some friends he helped. We also learned that my uncle himself delivered many messages, traveling with forged papers. This explained his frequent trips and unexpected family visits. To lessen suspicion, we were told, he openly befriended German officers or plain soldiers who came to his shop to buy pastries. He offered them coffee and engaged in long conversation during late afternoons while Maquisards slipped in or out of his shop through a back door. This behavior, unfortunately, mystified the neighbors for a long time.

Luckily, his wife and young son were never arrested. In time they sold the patisserie and moved away.

I never forgot my Uncle Raymond. His image stays young and spirited in my mind. Like the rest of the family, I admired him. I admired his drive, his success in branching out away from the farm, in such a different field as pastry-making. He looked so happy. Youthful, mischievous, with curly blond hair and sparkling blue eyes, he even stood apart physically from all his brothers and sisters, who had slightly darker complexions. His enthusiasm and spontaneity attracted everyone.

Like so many others, he lost his life by helping those who fought the enemy clandestinely, and in the process gave my family its own war hero. As for me, I will forever remember the colorful little pastries that came out of his oven, and how thrilled I was the first time he sent me all alone, to choose and fill a large tray of those delectable treats for our dessert after our usual late dinner. I loved my Uncle Raymond.

Chapter 19

D- Day.

"Bourges is burning! Bourges is burning!" the farmer screamed. "Come and see!" We ran out of the kitchen and joined him at the end of the yard where we had a clear view for miles around. Then we gasped at what we saw: the horizon was in flames! "Oh, no!" I exclaimed. "My parents are over there. What's happening to them? What's happening to my town?"

It was summer, 1944, and Michel and I worked at the farm again. So did Lucienne. This time when the farmer showed up at our door requesting our help, not only did my mother let my brother and me go, but begged the farmer to take our younger sister, too. I suspect the two of them had kept in touch with each other, as our bundles of clothes and things were already packed.

"You'll be safe there," my mother kept telling us. And my father had agreed.

There had been unrest in my town. It started on June 6, when the rumor spread that the Allied forces had landed on the coast of Normandy. The newspaper gave no hint. It only reported what the Germans wanted us to know, but someone listening clandestinely to a London broadcast had heard the news. And the words traveled from household to household. Most people had radios at home, but no one dared listen to overseas broadcasts, as it was strictly forbidden and very dangerous. German patrols easily tracked down anyone tuned to London and shot on the spot with no mercy, whoever happened to be there. Only brave people like the Underground communicated that way with London, always from hidden places in the woods or the back room of an isolated house, with someone on the lookout.

"*Le Débarquement a commencé!*" (The invasion has started) the man had shouted.

Such announcement should have made the townspeople jump with joy, but it did not. At least, not at first. Four years of brutal oppression had left them numb and spiritless, with no energy to spare. In the streets or stores, we only saw stern faces: no laughter, no loud talk. Apathy and resignation prevailed everywhere. So many young people had died already trying to fight the Nazi regime. Besides, they remembered hearing similar news a few years past, only to be deeply disappointed soon after. The German Army seemed unbeatable.

At home, my parents had stopped saying little phrases like, "When the war is over," and Michel and I did not have the heart to talk about what we would like to do "When we grow up." It seemed futile to plan for the future. We just tried to stay alive day by day. My brother talked more and more about quitting school and going to work somewhere to earn extra money so I could buy more food on the black market. He never had enough to eat.

I remember one time when my mother invited me for a short walk through town with her good friend Louise.

"It will cheer you up," she explained. "Monique and her brand new baby will be there, too," she added, trying to win me over.

"A happy reunion at last," I thought, and gladly went along.

Instead, I soon noticed with sadness that the two friends, usually bubbling with enthusiasm, behaved like everyone else: no spark, no smile. It seemed painful for them to talk and their voices stayed dull. They were repeating the news of the day: more civilians killed somewhere by air raid, more Maquisards caught and shot, more harsh measures and restrictions for the rest of the population. Demoralizing news as usual. I followed them with my head down, my shoulders crushed under a heavy load, and feeling something tight gripping me inside. My country was hopeless. The gloomy weather did not help; the downtown streets were deserted and my whole body felt cold. I remember cutting short the outing that day to go home.

But somehow the incredible news of the *Débarquement* slowly seeped through the lethargy of the people. Groups of German soldiers had been spotted leaving. Overnight, houses occupied by German officers were suddenly vacated. Soldiers or guards failed to appear at factories, like the one where my mother worked, and then finally entire bodies of troops were seen marching away.

"Where are they going? What's happening? Could it be true that the Allied Forces have landed?" People started to wake up and talk more openly.

Then gunfights erupted in the streets, in buildings, and on the highways. The Resistance suddenly came out of hiding, and under Charles De Gaulle's command, fought in the open, at every corner and every street, flushing out the remaining German soldiers wherever they found them. They liberated the schools, the hospitals, the villages around us and finally my whole town. We could hardly believe it.

My parents, hearing gunfire close by one day, sat around the kitchen table in silence, waiting. Their door was closed, but not locked as usual during daytime hours. They heard heavy running in the courtyard. Their door sprang open. A German soldier escaping from the farm up the hill had pushed it open, and came in, pointing a gun at my parents, but before anyone could move or scream, another shot was heard and the soldier dropped dead, right there, on the doorstep of my house. The Maquisard who had chased him relentlessly and finally killed him dragged his body away. But Grand-mère, our ailing friend who spent years caring for us through so many hardships, suffered a heart attack moments later, probably caused by the shock, and consequently died.

Of course, my mother had not waited for all of this to happen before sending my brother, sister and me to the farm. She anticipated the upheaval ahead of time, and did not even let us finish the school year. We had been at the farm for over a month before we heard of big battles happening everywhere around us. The friendly Maquisard who came regularly at the farm to get his food had kept the farmer informed of what was going on in Normandy and the rest of the country, before he, too, went on to fight somewhere. We knew the Germans were retreating. But we also knew that, before withdrawing, they took time to destroy whatever they were forced to leave behind. Horrible stories reached us. We heard that defeated German soldiers running away would choose at random any house standing on their path and viciously set it on fire, and then shoot the occupants as they tried to escape. It happened to one of my classmates.

I do not remember her name, too many years have passed since then, but I still visualize her face, so young and so pretty. She and her parents lived in a small house off a highway in the country, the same highway where Michel and I crouched under tall grass once, to watch the invading Germans march toward our town. Her house and ours stood a mere kilometer away, then.

That fatal morning, she went to visit her friends in the small farm across the road, that farm where I had found an egg in the bushes one day, and had grabbed it like a rare treasure. As she was preparing to return home, she heard soldiers approaching. She went back inside and hid in an upstairs room with her friends, waiting for the soldiers to go by. To her horror, from the window, she saw the Germans stop and surround her own house, drench it out with some liquid and set it on fire. It only took a few minutes. My schoolmate saw her mother run out screaming and fall down, shot by the soldiers. Then it was her father's turn. Her younger brother was found later, burnt to death, inside the house. My friend lost her whole family and saw her house burned down by German soldiers determined to destroy and hurt as much as possible before they, themselves, would be forced to surrender.

And there we stood, Michel and I, in the farmer's yard, out in the country where we were working for the summer, watching flames that reached the sky, far away in the distance. What was burning?

A few days later when the flames were finally subsiding, another farmer informed us: "It's the military base and the airport just outside of Avord. That's what is burning."

So it wasn't Bourges itself. I was relieved to hear my town had been spared. Avord was a little town standing a few kilometers southeast of Bourges. For two long days I had been worried about my parents' welfare. Did we even have a house to go back to? The farmer understood our anxiety and offered for us to stay at his home for as long as we wanted. Even years. Another long month passed and my mother finally came to take us home.

"No more German soldiers!" she said. "Only those who have been captured and who are now our prisoners of war."

Could it be possible? We had waited so long for such a day. Could it really be over in one summer?

I went home and found hundreds of French men and women scavenging through abandoned German headquarters for things that could be used again: desks, chairs, beds, cots, blankets, even food. My father explained the French were only taking back what had been theirs in the first place. Our own ration cards were discarded. Every week, food showed up more abundantly in the stores. Our bread became white again. "Too white," my father remarked. But we had plenty of it.

The war was still going on elsewhere in France, but in my town, it was nearly over. In the fall of 1944, the newspapers announced the arrival of Americans. They were supposed to cross our town on their way north to Paris, the very next day in early afternoon. School was in session that day, and no student was given permission to leave early to cheer and greet the soldiers. We were trying to catch up on our studies because we had missed so much already, when we had been forced to share our classes with other students whose school had been requisitioned by the German soldiers. Besides, for the last four years, we had been told over and over again to stay away from soldiers. So, I was in class the day the Americans came to my town and I never saw them. They just marched through our streets on their way to Paris. No battle. No fanfare. My town had rid itself of the enemy on its own, taking advantage of our allies forcing a great number of German soldiers to leave and join the fight on other fronts.

  D-Day and its following months proved rather quiet for me. I never witnessed the big battles in the streets. My parents did. I never saw people being shot in front of me. I only heard of it, so many times. My parents kept showing me the spot where the German soldier dropped right there on their doorstep, shot dead by a Maquisard. So close to them! My trips for food to the countryside became, of course, unnecessary, and ironically I missed them. I missed the sense of danger, I missed the excitement of outwitting the German patrols and I missed the great feeling of being useful to my family.

  D-Day brought the end of air raids and the freedom of walking at night without the fear of being arrested or shot. The trains resumed their regular and precise schedule and I could visit my grandmother anytime I wished. Life became more normal in my region even if the war was not completely over yet.

Chapter 20

A Moment of Truce

"Yugoslavs!" One of my neighbors exclaimed. "I am sure they were Yugoslavs. I recognized their accent."

"No! You are mistaken. They looked Polish to me," another retorted.

My neighbors were deliberating over the nationality of a large family who had been living at the end of our building since the beginning of the war, but who had abruptly skipped away a few days ago when most of the neighborhood was either at work or at school. They all agreed, however, on how relieved they felt that the foreigners had gone. For the past two years, we all had lived in fear of displeasing any member of that family and for good reasons.

The trouble started when the oldest daughter, a striking blond statuette, decided to live on her own because she had found a good job downtown. Exceptionally loyal to her parents, she visited them regularly. Before long though, she boldly showed up accompanied by a large group of rowdy young German soldiers. They arrived in jeeps, carried many bags of groceries and other packages, and made a lot of noise. We could hear their loud laugh from the other end of the yard even after they had entered the apartment and close the door behind them. My mother, fearful that my brother would do something foolish again, kept him inside the house on those days. Obviously, those neighbors were very friendly with the enemy, therefore dangerous, and my own parents tried very hard to stay away from them.

So, imagine our panic when the man in this family, a tall, slender, handsome specimen, but an enemy collaborator nevertheless, suddenly appeared on our doorstep one late afternoon. As usual on all sunny days, our door had been kept wide open to let the warm air come in, and to make the house more inviting to any passerby who wished to come in for a chat. We also liked to hear the happy sounds of the neighborhood children playing in the yard.

The man announced himself with a couple of knocks on the door but did not wait for an answer. In two steps he reached our table where we were still sitting after finishing our dinner. He seemed to be in a good mood, chuckling and talking vivaciously, in broken French. Puzzled, we looked at him, wondering what he really wanted. After a while, my mother finally guessed: "I know," she said, while walking to our medicine cabinet. "Which boy is hurt?"

My father had resumed his work at the distillery. Every now and then he brought home a little bottle of pure white alcohol distilled from plants (beets, usually). We used it as antiseptic on cuts and scratches as we had nothing else. It burned terribly for a few seconds on open sores but it worked magically and stopped any infection. The neighbors borrowed it frequently. My mother had understood correctly that our visitor wanted the bottle of alcohol.

He did. But to her horror, she saw him pull two small glasses out of his pocket, fill them up quickly, and raise his own as in a toast while offering the second one to my father. "No! You can't drink that poison. It will destroy your stomach," my mother gasped.

No one listened. The Yugoslav man did not hear or care for the warning. He swallowed the dreadful liquid in one gulp and filled another shot glass before my mother ever finished her sentence. The most horrifying thing is that my father did the same. The scene became hilarious in no time. Our visitor started to sing in his native tongue, my mother kept screaming and my father wanted to dance! Complete bedlam! My brother and I had never seen our father so relaxed, so talkative, and so happy. We did not even know he could dance and there he was, waltzing on the kitchen floor, pulling my mother round and round, while she called out: "Stop, Felix. Stop!" Strangely, it felt good to see our parents act that way and we kept watching. We even giggled and clapped with enthusiasm. Eventually, my mother put an end to everyone's happiness by throwing our neighbor out and scolding my father who fell asleep shortly afterwards. Then she hid whatever was left of the bottle.

Later, the men (my father and his quasi-new friend) chuckled whenever they met in the yard and even talked for a few minutes. Somehow, the foreign family did not seem quite as frightening. I myself did not hesitate to enter their house one school day, when one of their sons, a boy my age, asked me to help him with his homework. He had difficulty writing a French composition. His mother, who did not speak French at all, was all smiles over us during the whole time and rewarded us with a big bowl of vegetable soup as soon as we finished writing. Happy to have helped a new friend and my hunger satisfied by the thick barley soup, I raised my head and stretched my back against the wall, ready to chat some more, while my eyes wandered around.

That's when I saw it! The green uniform draped over the back of a chair. The color was unmistakable. German! I felt a chill. The sewing kit lay close by on the table. Shiny gold like buttons made a little pile next to it. Undoubtedly, the nice lady was repairing a German uniform. Was the soldier waiting in the back bedroom? I wondered.

Suddenly, her house did not feel so comfortable anymore. I left quickly.

The social moments never had the chance to repeat themselves. A few weeks later, the glamorous daughter vanished. So did her companions. The rumor is that she followed the soldiers when they started to retreat, fearing harsh retributions for her behavior if she stayed in town. Then the rest of the family disappeared, too.

Still, this unexpected visit from our Yugoslav (or Polish) neighbor, a man we used to fear, became an amusing event we liked to remember if only to tease my father and bring a smile to his face. To our chagrin, Michel and I never succeeded in making him waltz again as freely and happily as he did on that unforgettable evening.

Chapter 21

Our Grand Mazières

A quiet routine had returned to Grand Mazières, the little hamlet where we lived. The nights went undisturbed—no more air raids. No excuse for being late at school in the morning or feeling sleepy. Claude, the boy next door who had told me once how much he hated a clear blue sky as it surely attracted deadly warplanes, was now learning to appreciate warm sunny days. Children played at length in the yard at all hours of the day. The adults developed the habit of getting together outside on weekends, till late in the evening. No need to rush home simply because it was dark. The Germans were gone. So were their rules.

Le Grand Mazières remained a child's paradise. It had everything: a stream, a pond, a canal with tug boats that were pulled by donkeys, a lock, a farm, an abundance of trees and gardens and a punctual little commuter train that ran twice a day on the railroad tracks nearby. Farther away, the river where all the neighborhood children learned to swim lingered quietly before getting lost in a reservoir. Our own building had been a gristmill some time past, with the wheel fitting right under my mother's bedroom. We discovered the clue when we crawled through an opening underneath our house, next to the pond, and found a small oval room, like a tunnel with dirt floor and closed at one end. The rounded ceiling and walls were made of stones. A perfect little hiding place which I used occasionally, even though it felt too damp and spooky to linger in too long.

Young children were happy at Le Grand Mazières. They could explore all day long without ever getting bored. In hot weather, they waded in the stream collecting shiny stones or tried to catch small fish with hand-made traps. They chased the little ducklings waddling around and watched the cows taking their drinks at the end of the day, when the farmer brought them back to the barn after having let them spent the whole day in a pasture.

The stream was useful to everyone. Housewives did their weekly laundry in it. Bent over a big board where they scrubbed every piece of cloth with a brush and a square bar of soap, they plunged their hands in the icy water over and over again to shake any soap residue from the garment. In wintertime, their hands stayed red and swollen for days.

And then, the stream served another purpose: it cooled wine bottles in the summer time. Every household had its special dock. The bottles were laid down very securely between large stones so the current would not dislodge them, and were retrieved later at dinnertime by their individual owners. No bottle was ever stolen, lost or broken. The small children knew to be careful not to hit them with their pebbles and the teenagers ignored them entirely.

The Grand Mazières had another surprise: it enjoyed a castle, called appropriately, Le Château du Grand Mazières (the castle of Grand Mazières). Looking more like a tall manor house, it rose amidst gardens and trees, straight behind our back yard. A long time ago, it included all the land and buildings that still carried its name. During the occupation, German officers had been seen strolling on the grounds, but now the real owners were back and a gardener trimmed and raked every day, bringing order to the landscape.

One morning as we, the children of Grand Mazières, were walking to school, we noticed a lady standing beside our path, just outside the castle's side gate. She signaled us as we approached: "Wait!" she called out as soon as we reached her, and then she came straight to us. A little girl stood at her side. "*Bonjour*," the lady said.

"*Bonjour*," we replied, a bit curious.

"Would you let my daughter walk to school with you every morning from now on?" she asked. "She doesn't know the way and is a little afraid," she added.

"Of course," we replied with enthusiasm.

And so, in the true French philosophy where the rich and poor mingle together at times with perfect ease and even share the same community, we started to go back and forth to school with a little girl who owned a castle. It fascinated us. To our disappointment though, we were never invited inside the glorious premises. In time, the little girl quit the public school and left us. But by then, the castle had strangely become the weekend playground of a group of girls from the Catholic orphanage of our town. We could hear their joyous cries echoing a mile around.

And we saw Germans again. But this time, they wore a different uniform: striped prisoner of war uniforms! Some of those prisoners were sent to the farm where we still bought our milk. We saw them every day, usually at night when they came back from working in the field. They looked pitiful, with their heads held down as they crossed our yard. They did not dare look at us. We noticed a very young one, teenager-like. Michel could not resist meeting him.

As my brother strolled around the farm one late evening, he found the young, defeated soldier sitting against the wall outside, smoking a cigarette. Michel simply went to sit next to him without saying a word. He could not speak German anyhow, as the French population had never been forced to learn the language. Somehow, the two developed a friendship, meeting nearly every evening at the same spot. They managed to communicate. Michel learned the teenage German prisoner had lost all his immediate family when his house was destroyed by an air raid over Berlin. He had no one and no place to return to, if the war ever came to an end.

One bright afternoon, I came home early from school, and as soon as I entered my courtyard, I knew something big had happened. The women were dancing! Some were jumping. All were shouting. A frenzy was in the air.

"The war is over! The war is over! Germany has capitulated," they kept telling each other.

"The war is over?" I repeated to myself. "Is that possible?" It sounded so unbelievable that it left me numb.

Slowly, I walked across the yard toward the end of the building, trying to find a quiet spot where I could sort my thoughts out. Around the corner, I heard someone sobbing. There, all curled up against the wall, like a small bundle shaking all over, was one of my neighbors, an Italian woman. I went to her.

"What's wrong?" I asked. "The war is over. The news has been heard on the radio," I added, trying to comfort her.

"I know," she answered. "I am thinking about my younger brother. He was killed a month ago, back in Italy. He had been drafted in the army just before the war ended and was forced to fight the Allies. I tried so hard to bring him here, into France, but my request was always refused. If only he could have held on a little longer," she went on, sobbing some more.

But it was over. Really over. Our own prisoners of war were coming back. The girls living at the lock house saw their father again. My

Uncle Patrick, from Villefranche-sur-Cher, also returned from Germany. Our good friend Louise finally embraced her husband, too, and then introduced him to his new grandchild, a beautiful, blond little girl. And our teacher from the countryside, arrested and tortured by the Gestapo, miraculously survived it all and received a hero's welcome in his village. The family friend Louis, who had been sent along with my father to stop the German invasion at the onset of war but who had never returned, was back in town. As we had suspected, he had been captured. He also had been wounded, and because of a lack of prompt medical care, had lost a leg. It left him bitter.

For weeks, something more horrible made the news. A woman surfaced. She and her husband had disappeared from their neighborhood more than a year before. Even their closest friends were in the dark about their whereabouts. Then, the poor woman told her story to the authorities.

She and her husband had been part of the Underground. Captured by the Gestapo, they both had been inhumanly tortured until they collapsed. Her husband was the first one to die. She herself, extremely weak and mangled, was presumed dead. Their bodies were thrown into a truck, carried away to a distant field and dumped into a dry well. She landed on top of other bodies, which softened her fall and she spent the whole night there, praying to die quickly. Still alive the next morning, she managed to crawl out with whatever strength she had left, and went into hiding.

When the war finally ended and she was sure the Gestapo had gone, she led the French authorities to the well. The first body they retrieved was that of her own husband. A search for abandoned wells went on for months all over the region. More bodies were excavated. This, we learned, is how the Gestapo disposed of all the people they tortured and killed.

Then, for the first time, we heard of other horrible death camps: Dachau, Buchenwald, Auschwitz, where entire Jewish families perished. The sound of those names still brings chills to everyone's spine even after so many years. I thought of my two classmates who vanished overnight the year before. Did they meet their fate in those concentration camps? I will never know.

Yes, the war was over, but healing would take a long time. Our towns were destroyed, our spirits wounded, and thousands upon thousands of people had left us forever. This is why we kept our doors and windows wide open so we could hear the lively sounds of young children at play.

This is why we grew flowers and brought them inside to decorate our desolate homes, so our eyes could marvel at something beautiful again, despite the rubble. And this is why, to this day still, the French people love to gather with friends and family, at home or in open cafés, on sidewalks or small squares, and talk, laugh, enjoy each other's company, happy to feel alive again and tell the whole world.

Chapter 22

The Twists and Turns of my Teenaged Years

The year I turned fourteen, I fought my mother nearly every day to let me finish school. She had lost her job at the factory when the Germans left and for a little extra income took care of a boy toddler on a weekly basis. The boy's mother worked odd hours in the city and came only on Sunday afternoons to visit her son. This little boy soon became everyone's responsibility, sometimes even a burden for my sister and me. Our mother constantly requested our help.

"I have errands to do in the morning," she would casually tell us, "and I need one of you girls to stay home tomorrow and watch Charlie," as we called the new little member of the family.

To escape the chore I always thought of an excuse, like a school test or any other important activity in my class. Lucienne, growing up fast, inevitably volunteered and therefore missed a lot of school days. Before long, she quit going to school altogether to stay home and care for Charlie, therefore solving my mother's problems and mine. Michel too, eventually, dropped out of school when he reached the young age of thirteen and went to work full time in a factory nearby. My mother eagerly grabbed his wages, leaving him very little to spend.

"Food is expensive and you eat a lot," she justified herself. My mother was so impatient to see all her children earn a living, she nearly succeeded in making me quit school earlier too.

Graduation was approaching. Michel had made a little extra money working at odd jobs and wanted to give me a gift ahead of time. So one early morning at his request, the two of us rode our bicycles to a distant town where he had heard a shoe store was having a big opening. There, he helped me choose the prettiest pair of dressy shoes, those with a little heel, and proudly paid for them with his hard-earned money, knowing my mother would inevitably take whatever was left. Both of us felt exhilarated about the escapade until we faced our mother's anger at our return.

"Don't ever do this again!" she scolded my brother. "Odette has no use for that type of shoes. She is still going to school and has no job, therefore no need for fancy things. You foolishly spent money I could have used for more practical things."

My mother was furious that day and blamed me for what had happened. Without my knowledge, she went on to offer my immediate services to a young couple living in a boat on the canal. They needed someone to watch over their young children in the cabin below while they worked on deck or directed the boat. My mother would collect my salary each time they passed our lock.

"I found a job for you," she informed me abruptly one afternoon as I returned from school. The owners of the barge you see over there, docked on the canal, would like to hire you to care for their two children. I already talked to them; it's all arranged and you can start tomorrow."

Shocked, I could hardly talk at first. Seeing the disbelief on my face, she added with some authority: "Your grandmother grew up that way and never complained. Besides, you'll enjoy gliding on the water when the weather is hot."

At times, my mother acted like my enemy. Finally, my voice came back and I cried with anger: "No!" I screamed, feeling completely outraged. "I like school and would like to graduate. I will not go on that boat."

I had never answered my mother so bluntly before. She looked at me in surprise for a few seconds, then added, trying to convince me: "We sure could use the money."

I knew my parents were poor. I could see the worry on my mother's face when extra expenses came up unexpectedly, and I really intended to help eventually, but at the moment, graduation was more important. So, I stubbornly refused to meet the young couple and their children or even take a walk to their boat, and instead begged my mother to let me finish the school year. It took a while but she finally conceded, and from then on, never asked me to stay home for any reason on a weekday.

Not only did my mother let me graduate that year, but also as a reward, she gave me permission to visit my cousins in the town of Orleans.

"A train ticket is in the mail," I was told. "A gift from your aunt," she added. "Your cousins are asking for you."

Because I knew I was doomed to work somewhere as soon as my mother would hear of a place for me, I had asked Jeannine's older sister to help find a beginner's job for me in the dressmaking shop where she herself was happily employed as an apprentice. She did, and I expected to start in the fall, after the summer vacations. With a few weeks of free time ahead of me, I gladly took off for Orleans.

On my way there, though, I felt a little apprehensive. I had stayed at my aunt's house once before, during the Nazi occupation and had returned accusing her husband, my Uncle Gaston, a jovial and easy going man, of being a collaborator. He and my aunt ran a café restaurant on the outskirts of town. Workers from a factory close by came to have lunch every day. So did the German guards and my uncle greeted them like they were royalty. He served them his best wine, his best food, and he sat at their table and entertained them with his newest jokes. My ears still resonated with the sound of their laughter. He practically ignored the French customers. My aunt however, served those Frenchmen diligently. I had left, feeling horrified.

But when I confided my suspicion to the rest of the family, I was assured that my uncle's wining and dining of the enemy was a mere façade. It was his way of holding the soldiers as long as he could without endangering his own life, while the Resistance sabotaged the railroad tracks running in front of the restaurant. This delayed the flow of goods manufactured in the factory from going straight to Germany. Sometimes the wagons stayed stranded on the tracks for months. Still, I was not convinced. This friendly uncle seemed to enjoy his role too well. He developed an undying friendship with a German officer, a surgeon, who compassionately operated on my girl cousin, born with a cleft palate. This skilled German doctor restored my cousin's speech and smile, free of charge.

As I walked into the restaurant on my second visit, I heard my uncle talk and joke as usual with a group of workers. One man was patting him gently on the back while pointing to the railroad tracks we saw outside. "You sure helped us do a lot of damage," I heard him say.

"Yeah!" echoed the others.

"Remember the day you kept them drinking?" he went on, "Well, that gave us plenty of time to finish the job, and the trains did not get anywhere for weeks. Did they?" the man continued.

"No," another man answered. "And the goods lingered right here at the factory for a long time."

This bit of conversation stopped me from thinking any further about my uncle's loyalty, and I ran to give him a kiss on both cheeks. The workers applauded. They were in a festive mood.

"It's your uncle's birthday," my aunt explained, while serving coffee.

The celebration lasted until late in the evening with friends dropping in constantly. My two cousins and I giggled in the corner as we planned our next day and the ones to come. Altogether, I had a wonderful vacation that year, roasting new potatoes in the kitchen with my aunt or bringing bottles of wine to the bar for my uncle and enjoying the evening with my cousins and their friends.

When I returned home, more wonderful and astounding news awaited me. In my absence, a man I had never met had incredibly turned my future around. My parents and brother gathered around me that evening as soon as I arrived, and with excitement, tried to tell me something by talking all at once: "He had all the papers ready for us. We only had to sign at the spots he had marked. He checked your grades, and assured us you could get a scholarship to cover all expenses."

" Ecole Professionelle de Jeunes Filles," Michel repeated. "That's your new school and you start next Monday!"

I was baffled, unable to understand what they were talking about. "What do you mean? I have to start my new job next week," I mumbled.

My father, usually so calm, nervously stretched a piece of paper in front of my eyes and said:

"Look!" I did and recognized the name of the school my brother had just mentioned written in big letters, and the word "admitted" following my own name.

This time I was dumbfounded. "What happened?" I asked, looking at Michel. "What made the change of plans?"

"An earthquake," he answered with a giggle. "A real tour de force," he added with an air of mystery.

"Could you explain?" I asked again, while sitting down.

Finally, slowly, the three of them took turns telling me the whole story. It went as follows: A new man had appeared in the neighborhood. He had introduced himself as Monsieur Baillard, the youngest and most recent son-in-law of an older lady who lived in the row of houses across the yard. Apparently this lady was very sick and both Monsieur Baillard and his wife had moved in to take care of her.

At first, my parents listened to him with interest. The man spoke intelligently and seemed to be very informed about the politics of the time. He also was eager to help and wished he could improve the livelihood of every worker. All their lives, my parents had shied away from any kind of political discussion, as they never felt educated enough to understand the issues. This stranger made them feel comfortable, so they accepted the pamphlet he gave them. To their horror, later that evening, they realized the paper was a Communist newsletter and Monsieur Baillard, an ambitious politician, worked for the Communist Party. In fact, every week, Monsieur Baillard took the habit of distributing his propaganda pamphlets to every household in the neighborhood. My parents, intimidated and troubled, accepted the pamphlet to keep the peace, but threw it away immediately in the wastebasket.

At that time, my town was in political turmoil. After the Germans left, a temporary government had been quickly formed. But then came the moment for complete new elections and the Communist Party, big and powerful, was campaigning very aggressively. It already had succeeded in electing its own candidates in the surrounding villages, now governed by Communist mayors. People were coerced into voting or being penalized.

"Imagine our anxiety," my father continued the story, "when this Communist man barged into our house again, without being invited. He had knocked on the door slightly but pushed it open right away and walked straight to the kitchen table where he displayed the documents he was brandishing in his hand."

"I was sure they were more Communist propaganda papers," my father added, still looking disturbed at the thought of that evening.

My mother had felt frightened as well. She was aware of the violence that the Communists resorted to, sometimes, to force people to vote.

But then, she heard the man say: "I know of your daughter Odette. I know she likes school and I think I can help. It won't cost you anything."

Intrigued, my parents listened more attentively, still questioning themselves silently: What is this man talking about, they wondered.

"I work for the education department," Monsieur Baillard went on. "I checked your daughter's grades and I am sure she can get a scholarship. I have the application right here with all the necessary papers and you only have to sign."

My parents, by now completely bewildered and confused, dared ask: "How do you know about our daughter?"

Monsieur Baillard laughed and said: "My wife! As you know, my wife grew up here, and she and Odette confided in each other many times."

It started to make some sense. My parents did know Christine, his wife. Even though the lady was much older than I was, they had seen us together a few times, chatting. They even liked her, as she had always been very pleasant with them.

"It won't cost you any money," the man reiterated, eliminating the main obstacle. "And Odette will get a better job once she graduates."

"Another graduation?" my mother lamented. "It's a long time to wait."

"Your building is crumbling," Monsieur Baillard continued calmly, without paying attention to my mother's comment. "Odette might possibly help you move out of here someday."

I do not know if my parents grasped the wisdom of what the man was saying, or if they simply became overpowered by his insistence, but they finally gave up and signed everything. And there I stood, dumbfounded, but with a new future.

It was my turn to meet Monsieur Baillard. This man had walked miles on my behalf, checked several schools, registered me in the most appropriate one and came armed with a bunch of papers, determined to persuade my parents to let me go to school another four years.

Who was he, and why? I asked myself, while walking to his house.

A slim, nicely dressed and very serious looking person answered my knock on his door. I just mentioned my name and was immediately pulled inside. I heard my host call out: "Christine! Here is our girl."

And turning to me, the same man added while shaking my hand:

"I am Monsieur Baillard and very happy to meet you." We walked to the kitchen where Christine was bent over a steaming pot on the stove. A nice aroma filled the room and made the atmosphere warm and enticing.

"*Bonjour*, Odette," Christine exclaimed when she saw me. Then she went on: "I am so glad to see you. I told my husband all about your struggle with your family and schooling and he decided to help. Did you know he was a schoolteacher before I married him?"

I recognized other relatives sitting around the table. They were sorting out a big pile of newsletters. I guessed right away what those were: I had seen one of them in my parents' wastebasket already. But I came to visit and tell my benefactor how thankful I was, so I sat at the table too, and helped them to sort. We chatted for a long time about everything but politics. They just wanted to know more about me and asked me to keep in touch, which I promised to do. It felt good visiting this young couple. They were educated and well spoken, and I felt attracted to them.

The mother-in-law, a recluse widow, passed away and Monsieur Baillard eventually settled in Paris. I saw him less and less, only on rare occasions when he and his wife, along with their newborn son, came to visit the relatives still living nearby. But for many years, I remembered "Mister Communist Man," as I called him in my mind then, and thanked him with all my heart for having changed my life.

I did start my new school, a forty-minute walk from home, and continued going to it faithfully for nearly five years. As I promised, I kept my grades up, so tuition and book fees would be reimbursed. This time, my mother had been on my side completely. A place had been cleared away in the room for me to study, at a pretty new desk. I don't know where my mother found the money to buy it. Giving me her staunch support, she stubbornly refused to listen to all the friends and family members who kept on telling her it was foolish to send me to school.

"A complete waste of time and money," they kept repeating. "Girls do not need an education, only skills on how to cook and raise children, so they can find a husband."

"Husband! That word again," I screamed mentally. I had been about ten years old when the old lady living with us then, straightened me out on the subject. Here is what she said: "Your father cannot possibly take care of you for the rest of your life, so if you want a house of your own some day, you will have to find a husband."

Her statement left me unhappy for weeks to come. I knew I was too skinny and sickly looking to ever find a husband. "What's going to happen to me?" I asked her. She had no answer.

I was happy (and lucky) to get "an education," even if it was only a high school education. Oh! But what a guilty feeling I sometimes had when I entered the yard on late sunny afternoons and found it empty, my siblings and their friends still hard at work in some factory. I was aware of my new nickname floating in the neighborhood: "The Princess" as some teenagers amicably called me. They thought I was very privileged to be able to go to school while they had to earn a living. We were all taking different paths and did not hang around together as much. Even the river failed to attract us as a group, as it used to on hot summer days. On weekends, we all went to separate activities.

Graduation came and I searched frantically for a job, so I could, at last, contribute to the family budget. "You look too young," I heard over and over again. "We need someone with more experience."

Feeling demoralized, I turned to my favorite teacher for advice. Mademoiselle Fabres knew my family because she had once taken the long walk to my house to check on my health when she thought I was suddenly losing weight.

She listened to my plea attentively then said: "You have to grow up, Odette, away from your family. Go and see the world." Then, she came up with an idea. "London!" she exclaimed. "London is the place for you."

"What?" I burst out. "Isn't that a bit far? How can I get there?" I was completely astonished.

But Mademoiselle Fabres was determined and shared her vision. "English is the language of the future," she explained. "I have heard of families in England who take in foreign students as mother's helpers, an au-pair sort of thing. In exchange for room and board and a small wage, the students help with the children and the household chores. It's a great way to learn a new language."

My mother's wish a few years back, I thought quickly. But London seemed more exciting than a canal boat and I trusted my teacher, so I listened with excitement.

Mademoiselle Fabres went into action immediately. In a matter of days she located a family in need of a student, raised enough money to pay my fare and my new wardrobe, and sent me away with a few recommendations: "Stay in England as long as you can. Come back only when our town is more prosperous. It is taking a long time to rebuild."

The year was 1950 and I had just reached my nineteenth birthday. On the day I left, my mother and I walked to the train station. I could hardly contain my enthusiasm while she looked so sad.

"Don't forget to change trains in Paris," she kept repeating. "Take the one going north, to Calais. Don't get lost. You'll probably get seasick on the boat across the Channel."

As the train slowly departed, she tried to keep pace with it for a few minutes, her hand stretched out, waving me good-bye. "Write often," she yelled, wiping her eyes.

I left the window, sat on my seat and nearly let go a cry of joy. Finally, I was on my own, going away, leaving my old neighborhood behind. I watched the last house disappear in the distance with no regret.

Chapter 23

London!

Oh! How I loved London! The theaters, the buses, the parks, the subway! And certainly the museums, where I spent so many afternoons. And all the little candy stores where I bought boxes and boxes of chocolates. I developed my first toothache eating those chocolates in a London movie theater. How I wished my parents could have been with me to see the abundance of everything in the big department stores. Lovely, exotic items were everywhere. And food, still rationed in England even after the war ended, was plentiful in the household where I lived.

I had a fight in that home with the family pet once—a gorgeous Siamese cat, and the complete pride of its owner. I forced him to share his filet of fish dinner with me, one late afternoon. Everyone had gone away for the weekend and I was in charge of simmering a fancy meal for this spoiled little friend. Fresh fish! Wonderful fresh fish just out of the sea. Back in wartime, I would have walked miles for such a treat. I apologized to Mister Siamese Cat for filching half of his gourmet meal that evening and hoped he would not tell his master the next day by eating too voraciously. He did not. The man came back bringing with him dozens of eggs, butter and fresh fruits. Had he gone shopping on the black market in the countryside like I used to do? I, of course, had walked on dirt paths with a baby carriage, always in fear of German patrols, while he rode in a car, on paved roads, free of enemy soldiers.

A foreign city is both exciting and challenging. A different language is spoken. I practiced strange new words at every opportune moment.

"Good afternoon!" I usually said to the merchants selling fruits at street corners.

"How much for this apple?" I would ask. Then, on to another cart farther down the street. "Two oranges, please, Sir." One word at a time,

I learned to converse. Sometimes, I joined an older person sitting alone on a bench in a park, and while we watched children navigate their little sailboats on the lake, I tried full sentences:

"What a lovely day! The sun feels so good," to which I always received a smile. Old people are patient and speak slowly. My pace. But even the Bobbies (policemen) were wonderful. They gallantly told me what movie was playing where, and how to get there.

I was living a real adventure, and I owed it all to my high school teacher, Mademoiselle Fabres. I wrote her a letter soon after I arrived to tell her how happy I was. I also wrote to my mother to assure her I did not get lost on my way to London but did get awfully seasick on the boat as she had predicted. I never knew the waves in the sea could be so rough. Altogether, the trip had been cumbersome. It had meant riding a train to Paris, another one to Calais, then a ferry across the English Channel and finally another train to London, my destination. Once there, a taxicab whirled me all across a lovely countryside, from Victoria Station to some little town in the suburbs.

I arrived at my new English family's home in time for their late afternoon tea, that first day. An array of small sandwiches and pastries spread on the table welcomed me. A teakettle started to whistle and a teapot found its way next to my cup. We sat and I had my first experience with a delightful beverage I had not known. We tried to talk, but had great difficulty communicating because of the language difference. I also felt tired, so the lady of the house took me to my room to rest.

What a lovely room! So spacious, with a large bed, a desk and other big furniture. A whole bedroom for myself. From the window I could see the front gate, the tiny winding path to the house, and the small lawn engulfed by shrubs. Shiny drops of water from a recent shower still lingered on the leaves, making the air feel fresh and clean. So much greenery everywhere! A soft and cozy chair in the corner caught my attention. I pulled it a little closer to the window and slowly sank into it, still in awe about my whole trip. Then, I drifted away into a sound sleep.

I stayed fifteen months in London, which I still think of as a fascinating town. So much to see! One day though, a letter reached me and I recognized Michel's writing. It said: "The Americans have landed next door. They took over a military base and an airport in the towns of Châteauroux and Déols, located only a few miles from Bourges. They are searching for people who can speak some English. Can you say a few words in that language? I picked up an application for you. Please come home, we miss you."

I missed my family, too. And this was probably the opportunity Mademoiselle Fabres had dreamed for me, so I filled out the application that Michel had enclosed in his letter and mailed it. Three months later, I found myself working among the most exciting, easy going, good-hearted group of soldiers I had ever met: the American GIs!

Chapter 24

APO 10, US Air Force

No, I did not join the American Air Force, even though I was tempted. I liked the uniform. I just worked for it as a French civilian. My interview went well, and I was granted a job right away in the communications department as a long distance switchboard operator. The pay was great and it felt exciting to call all the American military bases scattered over Europe. What a great way to practice my English.

I found one huge problem, though, at the beginning. On that first Thursday when I came to search for a place to live, I could locate nothing. All the apartments listed in the local newspaper had already been taken, usually by the latest arrival of an American family.

"The Americans are wonderful," a landlord told me. "They pay much more money for rent and then modernize the place."

The hotels, too, were full. Not one room available anywhere. "It's a bad weekend," I was told, over and over again.

"Every room is already reserved," a clerk assured me. What is going on? I wondered. There was no special holiday coming up, the town seemed quiet, and yet there was absolutely no vacancy in all the hotels I checked. It puzzled me.

A café stood at the corner. I was tired and hungry, so I went in for a bite to eat. The waitress brought me a wonderful, long, crusty sandwich. As I started to feel better, I looked around and noticed an attractive lady with a little girl two tables away from mine, looking at me with curiosity. As soon as our eyes met, the lady pulled a tote bag from under her seat. Then, showing off the large unmistakable London Bridge design imprinted on it while pointing to my own tote bag next to me, she exclaimed: "We have the same bag! Did you get it in London? We are just back from visiting that town."

Indeed, we had the same novelty handbag I had bought in a small London boutique. "Yes," I mumbled. "I guess we do. I lived over there for a while."

Eager to chat with someone, I stood up and walked to her table. I was amazed to see that she and her daughter were drinking tea, with lots of lemon. They offered me a cup and for an instant, I was back in England. We laughed when we found out we shopped in the same London district at about the same time. "What a coincidence," I remarked.

"Sure is," the lady added. "But what brings you to our small town of Châteauroux?"

"I have a job on the base, starting next week, but so far, it's been very discouraging. I can't find any place to live, not even a hotel room for tonight."

"And you won't!" the lady blurted out. "Not this weekend."

"Why not?" I exclaimed with anger in my voice. "That's the answer everyone is giving me. What's so special this weekend?"

"It's payday," the lady stated simply. Then seeing the confused look on my face, she went on to explain: "It's payday for the American soldiers. Starting tomorrow, they will come down in busloads from the base and invade all the bars and nightclubs—a big noisy drinking party. Dozens of prostitutes will arrive from everywhere for the occasion, mostly by trains from Paris, and fill up the hotels. That's why you can't find any lodging. The hotel managers anticipate the arrival of this lucrative clientele and save all their rooms for them. They get twice as much money on those days. The townspeople will again complain that the loud noise keeps them awake at night, but to no avail. As usual, the commanding officer on the base will quickly point out to our mayor that the town's economy is suddenly booming, therefore we should be happy. We are not. It is slowly creating animosity. Our young French men are forced to go elsewhere for entertainment as the waitresses often neglect them, while the American soldiers get all their attention simply because they tip much more generously. It's deplorable."

I was crushed. Still, I wanted to hear more, and the lady complied: "It's more than deplorable," she stated with indignation. "At times, it's absolutely disgusting. After such weekends, the town is filthy. The back alleys are full of vomit from the previous nights by those young, undisciplined soldiers who probably never drank wine before. In the morning, when the town residents leave their apartments to go to work, they have to step around piles of mess that litter the sidewalks, until the city sweepers finally come and clean it up. It's an ugly sight and we don't know what to tell our children."

The lady was out of breath. Obviously, she was happy to unload her resentment as she quickly went on, after a short pause: "During the whole Nazi occupation, I never saw an inebriated German soldier walk down the street, but I can't count anymore how many American GI's I saw passed out by the side of a bar. They need a curfew. I miss the regular army, the real soldiers who fought so bravely for us and commanded our respect. They were our heroes and we welcomed them. They went back home to the States for a well-deserved rest and are being replaced, unfortunately, by teenagers who have too much freedom, too much energy and waste it all on drinking."

I had heard enough and was getting ready to leave when she, again, caught my full attention by announcing: "I think I know a place where you can stay temporarily."

"You do? Where?" I practically screamed.

"There is a boarding school for young girls, not far from here, only a couple of streets behind this café. Sometimes, they have extra empty beds in their dormitory and let outside young women sleep there for a small fee. It's of course on a temporary basis and very limited. My daughter and I felt extremely grateful last year when they let us rent two rooms during the summer break. We too, could not find any apartment readily available when we first came to this town. The rules are strict, though: no noise, no radio and the gate closes early in the evening. Are you still interested?"

"Of course I am," I exploded. "It's my only chance."

"Let's go then," my new friend commanded.

It took five minutes to find the school, and when we rang the doorbell, a chubby woman came running to open the gate. She recognized my companions right away and greeted them both with a warm handshake. I followed the group into an office and let my new benefactor do all the talking. That night, I slept safely in a narrow but comfortable bed, all alone in an empty dormitory. A week later, when school reopened, a group of schoolgirls invaded my space, whispering and tiptoeing all around me.

It took over a month for me to find a room of my own in a private house. And that room was only available to me because no one else wanted it. Small, barely furnished, it had no indoor plumbing, no running water either hot or cold, and only one electric outlet. Its door, carved out of a niche in the thick wall of the stairwell about halfway between first and second floor, looked as inconspicuous as the entrance of a small storage room. Visitors were startled to discover someone lived there, behind those stone walls, when they heard the muffled sound of music escaping through, while they climbed the steps. In wintertime though, I had to choose between plugging in my radio (which I adored) or warming my room with an electric heater, (which I needed occasionally). A far cry from the luxurious bedroom I left behind in London! Nevertheless, after spending years in similar discomfort while growing up, it did not take long at all for me to accommodate myself all over again to the lack of plumbing.

Besides, I liked the old house with its shady garden, perched high on a hill from where we could peek out on the new part of town down below. The view was breathtaking. I also loved my new job, which kept me busy. The American GI's were pleasant to work with. Like every other civilian employed on the base, I made three times more money that the average French worker.

"*Uncroyable!*" (Unbelievable!) my father screamed when we compared paychecks.

My friendly "Mr. Communist Man" had been right all along. A few extra years of schooling helped me to get a better paying job. But as the lady from the café had predicted, I too experienced the noisy weekends. I usually tried to get away on those days, and visit my parents. But Monday mornings proved horrible when I had to walk down my street to the bus stop. I carefully walked through puddles of disgusting litter that smelled so bad that people kept their windows closed.

At long last, some order was established. The MP's (Military Police) began to routinely pick up the soldiers off the street before any of them collapsed from drunkenness and risked the extra humiliation of being robbed (and disrobed) while semi-unconscious. The hotel bar-restaurant, located only a few blocks away from where I lived and which had become a house of ill repute in a short time, was finally declared off-limits to the troops. From then on, my street stayed clean and peaceful.

My landlady was a wealthy, intriguing widow and grandmother. A title attached to her last name suggested that long, long ago, her ancestors might have belonged to the French nobility. Her living room overflowed with intricate objects of art, which came from far away places.

"Gifts from my great uncle, who made his career in the French merchant marine and traveled all over the Orient," she told me once, while I was admiring her numerous treasures.

The two of us spent many evenings chatting about anything. She was very fond of the Americans. I never heard her criticize the behavior of the turbulent young soldiers. I wondered why. Nearly half a century later, I discovered her big secret.

People grow old and pass away. My landlady did not escape her fate. When I went back for a visit around 1995, mostly out of nostalgia, but also to show my sixteen-year- old granddaughter the quaint little house where her father spent the first year of his life, I noticed a plaque recently put on the outside wall, next to the door. It started to say something like:

"In honor of the American paratrooper who found refuge in the basement of this house during the Nazi occupation, while helping the Underground."

I rang the doorbell, by impulse. The stranger who came to answer let me in after a brief introduction. When hearing I had lived on the premises shortly after the war while the last owner of the house was still alive, he besieged me with questions:

"Do you know how many rooms there are altogether in the basement? I just discovered an extra one last year. Do you know all the secret doors?"

In an instant I was magically thrown back to the time when my landlady (Madame Ravault de Verneuil) would ask me to escort her down to the cellar. In the first room, the only one with an electric switch and light bulb, she kept her harvest of fruits and vegetables, which she preserved for the winter. I helped her turn each one of them over gently in the straw, checking for any impurity. Then, we would explore the rest of the basement with a flashlight. My landlady would always find a passageway cut into what I thought was a bare wall, but which inevitably turned out to be a hidden door leading into another room, and then another. The last one was the darkest and gloomiest. Yet, we would stay there for a while, inspecting each wall carefully. Why? I still don't know. Was my landlady searching for another secret door? The three-story house was built nearly two hundred years ago, of huge thick stones, on a hill, and was still full of mystery.

I learned from the new tenant that the townspeople and its successive mayors spent years trying to locate the brave paratrooper from America. They found him in Texas, a couple of years before he, too, passed away. Bringing him back to this little French town, they honored him with a big parade and a day of celebration with some of his old friends from the Resistance. My landlady had never confided in me how she risked her own life by hiding an American during the Nazi occupation.

But I could not help noticing how delighted she became the day I introduced her to a young heart-warming GI who, six months later, became my husband. I remember how eagerly she invited me then to move immediately to her more spacious third floor apartment which had (would you believe it?) all the modern conveniences of that time.

I was married from that apartment. My fiancé and I rode two blocks to the *mairie* (mayor's office) to be first married by the town's mayor as required by the law. Then, we were allowed a longer ceremony in the church of our choice. Finally we drove all the way to Bourges, my home place, to celebrate all night long. A year later, the same apartment welcomed my first son, five days after he was born in the military hospital on the base. That same apartment would have witnessed my son's first step had we not gone on vacation on the French Riviera the week before. The sand, soft and warm, proved irresistible to him.

Altogether, I spent four years working for the occupying American Armed Forces. Summer 1956 came along and the Army did not give any hint of leaving. The cold war had started. Some French people feared the Russians would march straight to France to engage battle with the Americans and our country would get demolished all over again. Others, influenced by the numerous Russian movies that invaded our theaters and depicted the life, suffering and patriotism of the Russian people during the war, and sympathized with them, wished strongly that the Red Army would cross our border to dislodge the Americans who, they thought, had extended their stay. Allegations of rape, pregnancies, stayed unresolved.

"This particular airman is no longer stationed here. He has been transferred to another base and we are not responsible for him anymore," was the constant irritating answer from the American authorities.

A very confusing if not unsettling time. Yet, every week, the newspaper published announcements of marriage between French girls and American GI's. Romance flourished all over town, regardless of the politics.

My husband and I had bought a car early on so we could have door-to-door transportation when we visited my parents and all the other relatives. I remember the great entrance we made the first time we entered Grand Mazières, where the children thought only their familiar doctor had the privilege of owning an automobile. They all wanted a short ride, and my popular husband happily complied. My husband knew how to charm anyone. My parents could not resist his contagious laugh, his enthusiasm and his funny way of speaking French. My other relatives were attracted to him and competed in inviting us to their homes for a Sunday dinner. Even "Mr. Communist Man" shook his hand smiling curiously, one late summer evening, when I introduced the two of them. My husband was happy in France.

So, it was with both sadness and excitement that we said goodbye to friends and relatives one day, and told them: "Tomorrow, we go home to America."

We did. A few years later, my sister, Lucienne joined us. In no time, she found herself a husband. A Frenchman no less, who had spent years growing up only a few kilometers away from our grandmother's village, back in France, but whom we had never met. The couple settled in New York City where they eventually raised four children. Michel chose to stay behind in the town he loved: Bourges. He married and started a family of his own. After a long separation of seven years, my mother came for a short visit. She amazingly fell in love with everything she saw in this new land, (mostly I think, my washing machine and television, and all the friendly people she met at the park when taking her grandson, William, for a stroll). At her return, she persuaded my father to prepare for a permanent voyage to the USA. It took a few more years, but finally, New York City counted two more newcomers among its people. My American husband (who had become extremely fond of my parents), I and my new married sister, all contributed to successfully finding a place for them, where they lived happily and peacefully for the rest of their days.

I am making my First Holy Communion at twelve years old.

Michel's first Holy Communion around eleven or twelve years old.

Ecole Professionelle de Jeunes Filles, my high school.

I pushed my "black market" baby buggy along the canal to seek food for my family. Today the canal has been filled in to make a walking path.

Michel, eighteen years old, doing his military service after the war.

The stream La Rampenne which ran by our house in Grand Mazières.

Epilogue

Years have passed. I now have miraculously reached this segment of life where people my age are referred to as senior citizens. It's a glorious time. We leave the problems of the world to the younger generation. The days are quiet and peaceful, still full of activities. Gardening, playing bridge or hopping in the car to visit family and friends are among my favorite occupations. The young grandchildren occasionally keep me busy too, if not utterly exhausted, when I babysit for them. The weeks, months, even years, follow each other in a faster pace as I try to crowd my days into them.

I wrote this book at the request of my son, William, who, afraid that the stories he heard while growing up would fade away quickly as my human memory might start to fail, suggested diplomatically that I should solidly print them on paper. It felt good to relive the past and bring back alive all the people I used to know.

I want to thank all my friends who encouraged me to keep on writing by showing so much interest at every chapter, all at awe about the details of daily life under the Nazi regime during World War II. Some remembered uncles or fathers or even older brothers who fought in that war, but who remained reluctant to talk about it, and those friends were eager to know more.

I especially want to thank my invaluable friend, Lucille Worcester, who gave me her entire support, and through her sheer enthusiasm, prompted me to finish this endeavor. She read, edited, cried and laughed, all at the same time, while we sat together at the kitchen table many late afternoons, a strong drink in hand to help us glide over the most tragic moments.

I also want to thank my neighbor next door, Daniel Kolanowski, who gallantly rescued me each time I had a fit of rage with this modern gadget called a computer.

I am sorry to report I am no longer married with my carefree, fun loving American GI. After eighteen years of marriage, we amicably divorced (a disease of the time). My husband constantly reproached me for being too serious, "not fun enough," as he used to say. The tragedies of the war, I suppose, had left its marks on my behavior.

From time to time, I go back to France and revisit the places of my childhood. My old house in Grand Mazières no longer exists. It gently crumbled into the ground. The whole area has now been transformed into a man-made lake which people flock to on sunny days, joggers, especially. My beloved canal too, has disappeared. The big, large trees are still there, but the tranquil water, full of fish, is gone. It has become a large grassy promenade for those who still like to walk. Even the stream called La Rampenne, where I lost the family ration cards once, is now tunneled underground at places. The river where I learned to swim with all my friends looks so polluted I shudder at the thought I bathed and swam in its water with utter delight years ago. But the lovely gardens, even the ones where I gorged myself with strawberries, are still in existence, tended by patient, older gardeners who love to chat with curious passers-by like myself.

Writing this last paragraph makes me homesick. It's time to plan another trip, one last time perhaps, before my body and soul give up under the aching pressure of longevity.

"France, I hear your call!" my heart says. "Tomorrow, I will make some arrangements," my head answers.